improv for everyone

improv for everyone

greg tavares

© 2012 by Greg Tavares

ISBN-13: 978-0-9859507-0-5

Printed in the United States of America

Editors: Jessica Mickey & Colleen Reilly
Designer: David Mandel & Ampersand Industries
Proofreader: Sara Miller

Published by M&L Books
Charleston, South Carolina

All rights reserved. No part of this book may be reproduced, stored in a retrieval system, or transmitted in any form or by any means, electronic, mechanical, photocopying, recording, or otherwise without permission of the author.

Contents

SPECIAL THANKS	VIII
PREFACE	IX
CHAPTER 1: IMPROV IS ENOUGH	**1**
What Is Improv?	2
How to Use This Book	4
Talent vs. Technique	7
CHAPTER 2: STAGE 1 OF THE SCENIC STRUCTURE:	
THE NOODLES AND THE SAUCE	**10**
Say Yes to Saying Yes	13
The Three Stages of a Scene	16
Building a Scene Is Like Flying a Plane	20
CHAPTER 3: THE FIVE SCENIC ELEMENTS: CREPP	**22**
Character	26
Relationship	27
Environment	29
Point of View	30
Point of Attack	32
CHAPTER 4: THE JOIN	**34**
A Philosophy: You + Me = We	34
A Step-by-Step Method	36

CHAPTER 5: THE CLICK	**46**
How to Create the Click by Using "The Method"	49
CHAPTER 6: STAGE 2 OF THE SCENIC STRUCTURE: EXPLORING CHARACTER POINT OF VIEW TO DISCOVER YOUR PRIMARY EMOTIONAL DRIVE	**54**
Character Point of View: A Little Goes a Long Way	58
The Actor Disease	60
CHAPTER 7: STAGE 3 OF THE SCENIC STRUCTURE: HEIGHTENING	**63**
Heightening Point of View Using Relationship Componentry	67
Relationship Components and Environment	77
The Other Way to Heighten: Raising the Stakes	78
Why Do We Heighten?	81
The Problem with Heightening	83
CHAPTER 8: JUDGMENT, FEAR, AND COURAGE	**86**
CHAPTER 9: 11 HABITS OF HIGHLY SUCCESSFUL IMPROVISERS	**89**
CHAPTER 10: READ THIS BEFORE YOU START DOING THE EXERCISES	**101**
CHAPTER 11: WHAT TO DO, STEP BY STEP, TO CREATE AWESOME SCENES	**104**
CHAPTER 12: STEP 1: GETTING CONNECTED	**106**
The First Exercise: The Focus Push-up	107
More Exercises to Get Connected	113
CHAPTER 13: STEP 2: YES AND . . .	**121**
Exercises	122
CHAPTER 14: STEP 3: THE PRE-SCENE: THE FIVE-STEP METHOD AND THE JOIN	**128**
Exercises	133

CHAPTER 15: STEP 4: BUILDING THE AGREEMENT:
THE NOODLES — 138
Exercises — 140

CHAPTER 16: STEP 5: FINDING YOUR CHARACTER'S *How*:
THE HEAD, HEART, BODY METHOD — 146
The Head, Heart, Body Method — 148
Exercises — 150

CHAPTER 17: STEP 6: MAKING ENVIRONMENT SPECIFIC,
REAL, AND AUTOMATIC: THE WHERE-FOUR — 158
The Where-four (in no particular order) — 159
Exercises — 162

CHAPTER 18: STEP 7: ADDING THE SAUCE: RELATIONSHIP
AND POINT OF VIEW — 168
Relationship Componentry Exercises: Disclaimer — 171
Relationship Componentry Exercises: History — 172
Relationship Componentry Exercises: Emotion — 175
Relationship Componentry Exercises: Status — 179
Relationship Componentry Exercises: Physicality,
Sensuality, and Space — 193

CHAPTER 19: REVIEW OF STEPS 1–7 — 201

CHAPTER 20: STEP 8: BELIEVING YOUR WORLD — 204
The Click — 204
Sense Memory Exercises — 206
The Emotional Recall Technique — 212
The Substitution Technique — 215
Substitution Exercises — 217

CHAPTER 21: MICRO-TECHNIQUES — 223

CHAPTER 22: LONG FORM OR SHORT FORM?
NO NEED TO PICK ONE — 237

CHAPTER 23: ME, THEATRE 99, AND
HOW TO GET IMPROV TO LOVE YOU BACK — 241

Special Thanks

I would like to thank a few people. Without their help, this book would not have been possible: Anne Dreher for making me feel like I can do anything; Tice Miller for seeing something in me before anyone else; Jayce Tromsness for liking me doing improv even though he did not like me all that much; Brandy Sullivan for being the strongest partner I could ever hope to find; Colleen Reilly for reading these pages with loving guidance; my mother and father for supporting me without having to understand me; and my wife, Sara, for being my best friend and for improvising with me every day of my life.

Preface

Hello, reader. Welcome to my improv book. I hope you like it. I hope it helps you like what you do when you improvise. This is a how-to book, and my goal in writing it is to give you some tips and methods to make your improv more fun, effective, and satisfying. When I read how-to books, I look for tangible stuff I can actually use—even better, tangible stuff I can use today. When I read how-to books, I want immediate impact—I want to get better *now*. That is what I am trying to give you in this book.

First things first: Reading this book will not make you funny. A book can't do that, and what's worse is that, right now, as you browse this book for free, you are already as funny as you will ever be. If you just want to "be funny," this book and improv are not for you; so if that is your goal, put the book down and go somewhere else.

If you are still with me, I am going to assume that you are a lot like me when I started doing improv. You love improv and want improv to love you back. You enjoy improv most when you are in great scenes. When you are in great scenes, you feel a real connection with your scene partner and the audience, and you want more of that.

Okay, you are picking up a book to make yourself a better improviser, so you must feel like you have some room for improvement. Good.

This is the book I wish I had when I was just getting started and had no real guide. It's a book for people who love improv and want improv to love them back. You could try to figure out this improv stuff on your own, or you could just read this book. I've included pretty much everything I've ever learned over the past 25 years or so. This book will not make you funny, but it will give you step-by-step methods to create awesome scenes.

Chapter 1
Improv Is Enough

Who am I, and what insight can I offer you into the kick-ass art form of improv?

Here is the most important thing you need to know about me: I treat improv as an end, not as a means to an end. For me, improv is enough. Creating awesome scenes out of thin air with my partner is enough. I am not doing improv to achieve some other goal. Doing improv *is* the goal. I've spent over 25 years of my life doing it, and I still love the feeling I get when I look into my scene partner's eyes and have no clue what they are going to do next.

I love the freedom of it. I love the trust and support that true partnership demands, and I love that improv is pure collaboration. For me, the 100 percent collaboration of improv is thrilling because no one is in control. My partner and I set out to create something awesome, but we don't know what it is going to be and nobody is in charge. There is no leader, and there is no plan. In every other walk of life, this would be a recipe for disaster, but not in improvisation. It's this spontaneous collaboration that creates the freedom to play, make mistakes, and discover that keeps me coming back. That is why I keep doing improv—I just want to see what my partner is going to do next. That is my favorite part, getting to play with my partner, whoever they are.

That's the goal of this book. To teach you how to work with your partner, using only spontaneous collaboration to create awesome scenes—nothing more, nothing less.

Something else you should know about me: I am not famous, nor have I completed any of the big improv training programs. But I have done thousands of shows and taught a thousand classes, and this is what I do for a living. The shows I perform in and classes I teach have one thing in common—the people watching them and taking them are members of the general public, not improvisers or actors. The people sitting in the audience are people who could have, just as likely, gone to see Will Ferrell's latest movie, and the students in my classes are, for the most part, not actors, just people like yourself who came to improv by accident. I don't know how to teach you how to nail an audition for *Saturday Night Live* or write for *The Daily Show*, but I do know how to teach you how to do improv scenes for audiences who like to laugh. So this is your second warning: if you want to use improv to get an audition for *SNL* or develop stand-up comedy material then put the book down and go do that. If just doing improv is not enough for you, then this is not the book for you. But if you can be satisfied with spontaneously collaborating with your partner to create awesome scenes, then stick around, because that's what we are going to do.

It's time to begin.

What Is Improv?

Let's take a moment to talk about what it is we are trying to create when we say improv. First and foremost, improv is acting. Acting without a script. And as Charles McGraw put in his classic book by the same title, "Acting is believing." So, if improv is just unscripted acting, it follows that improv is just unscripted believing. Believing in the world of the scene that you are spontaneously creating before our very eyes.

People forget this all the time, but improv is basically just make-believe. Just like an actor in a play, film, or television show has to make-believe the situation written on the page is real, an improv actor has to make-believe the scene they create is real. The problem is that this almost never happens because everyone involved is usually so worried about being funny.

It is important to keep in mind that, fundamentally, your job as an improviser is to transform from yourself into a character and then to pretend or make-believe you are that character. What you transform into could be anything—a talking bear, a person at work reading their email, a high school football coach, whatever—it does not matter, but for a few minutes, you are going to be that character. Never forget that improv is simply believing that you are somebody you're not and pretending to do stuff you're not really doing. Improv is make-believe.

Not only is improv spontaneous make-believe, nobody knows what happens next. There is no plan. Everyone involved is just trying to figure out what the heck is going on, and I mean everyone—you, your scene partner, and the audience. I have seen hundreds of students pop out in the middle of a scene, look me straight in the eyes, and say, "I'm lost, I don't know what I'm supposed to do next," to which I reply, "Nobody knows." You can't know, and that is why it's called *improvisation*. If you knew what was going to happen next, it wouldn't be improv.

Sometimes when I tell students this, they realize that it's okay to be totally lost during a scene and have no clue what happens next, and they are deeply comforted. Sometimes the student, right then and there, overcomes their anxiety to "get it right." They start to "just play" and have fun. Sometimes it has the opposite effect and I never see the student again.

So, to recap, improv is just make-believe and nobody knows anything about what is going to happen in the scene; therefore, it is very important for the improv actor to actually believe in their make-believe. Remember, improv is acting and acting is believing—so go ahead and believe.

How to Use This Book

Here's how this book is going to work: First, I am going to discuss the big picture and my general improv philosophy, so you will know what I mean when I say "improv." Then, in later chapters, I will tell you how to do it. So, get ready for the big picture (chapters 1–10) and stand by for the methodology (chapters 11–21).

A word about my philosophy—my approach is very technical. You'll find that I break improvisation down into all the little steps one has to take in order to do it. For example, in the next few chapters, I am going to introduce a specific way of breaking down improv scenes—a scenic structure. I am also going to introduce a detailed way of looking at the relationship between characters in improv scene work. It may appear that I am breaking down scenes and relationships into their atomic particles. This is by design. Because I want you, the improv actor, to know exactly what you are creating when you improvise.

A word about my methodology: In chapters 11–19, I describe what I do, step-by-step, to create awesome scenes. These step-by-step methods will help you put into practice the improv philosophy outlined in this book. Some of these exercises and step-by-step methods may seem simple and childlike. This is also by design. My approach to scenic theory is technical, but my methodology is very easy to use and understand. As I say in my classes, "Big ideas, small steps."

When you start to apply the philosophy and step-by-step methods in this book, keep in mind that improv is a failure-based art form. It takes a long time to master new techniques in any field, and whenever you try something new, you will fail more often than you succeed. Think back to when you learned how to ride a bike. For some people, it was hard and took a while. You got some skinned knees in the process, and you looked kind of dorky when you were learning, but it was worth it. Riding your bike with your friends was fun, and the more you did it, the better you got. After a while, you could ride your bike without even thinking about how you were doing it. All the step-by-step methods you learned had become automatic. You still did them, you just didn't think about doing them. You can do the same thing with improv. The step-by-step methods can become automatic; you can do them without thinking about doing them.

What is difficult is that while you learn a new way of doing something, you make lots of mistakes. I say improv is a failure-based art form because inexperienced players fail almost every time they try to do a scene. When someone starts doing improv, it may be years before they are in a truly great scene. Improvisers need to recondition themselves to see failure not as a negative, but as a necessary step toward success. What's worse is that trying new approaches and methods when learning anything increases the potential for failure. So, here is the deal: improv is a failure-based art form, and when you try out a new way of doing it, you are going to fail more often than not, but you still have to stay positive.

Why?

Because negativity doesn't work. Being negative about yourself as an improviser will not make you a better improviser. Beating yourself up for doing a scene or show that you thought failed will not make you a better improviser. What will make you a better improviser is to stay positive while you keep trying new approaches and methods until you find the ones that work for you.

I have found that because improv is a failure-based art form, teachers often resort to telling improvisers what not to do instead of what to do. Faced with so many scenes that fall short, frustrated teachers try to limit their students' failure by creating rules for what not to do in improv scenes.

Here is the problem with that approach: you can't learn how to improvise by thinking about what not to do.

If you create rules for what not to do in your improv, you might reduce some of the failure, but you sacrifice some of the freedom. You create safer improv, not better improv, and it's less fun.

I have found that improv students are hungry for methods that outline what to do. That's what you take improv classes to learn, right? You want to learn what to do when you get up there and try to create a scene with your partner. Even though students are hungry for positive guidance, teachers give negative direction. They waste students' time by teaching them what not to do.

Here is a list of things teachers have told me, over the years, not to do when I improvise:

> Don't talk about what you are doing.
> Don't think.
> Don't use questions.
> Don't say the word *no*.
> Don't talk about the past.
> Don't talk about the future.
> Don't talk about characters who are not in the scene.
> Don't start the scene with a problem.
> Don't start at the beginning.

Don't, don't, don't—great, now I know what not to do, but what do I do?

I promise you, every time you truly succeeded at something—bowling a strike, getting a job, asking someone out on a date—your success was based on you doing something. You bowled a strike because you rolled the ball to just the right spot, not because you were thinking, "Don't make a mistake."

In this book, there are no *don't*s. No rules, only step-by-step methods that lead to scenes that, more often than not, succeed in making the audience care. This book will teach what to do, step by step, to create awesome scenes.

Some of the methods outlined in this book will work for you and some will not. My approach is very technical, and just like anything that has a step-by-step process, the first time you do it, it feels like walking through mud. Try to give yourself a little time to become familiar with each of these methods. I know we all want to just get out there and play, but sometimes adding some steps and form to the play can make it more successful and, therefore, more fun. I have the most fun doing improv when I am in awesome scenes and that is what the steps are there to help you create.

So, even if the step-by-step method I am outlining seems simple and childlike, try it anyway. Really, do it, and let the doing make you a better improviser.

Talent vs. Technique

If you are the kind of improviser who just goes from the gut and follows your inspiration every time you do a scene, then the step-by-step methods outlined in this book will seem redundant to you. Technique is for when you are uninspired—when, for the moment, your natural talent is not pushing you to do something specific to create an awesome scene. If you are just really talented, fearless, and constantly inspired, then you do not need this book. This book is for people who are not really talented, fearless, and constantly inspired but want to learn how to seem really talented, fearless, and constantly inspired.

Over the years, I have learned that it does not matter how you create your awesome improv scenes. You can use talent or training, fearlessness or courage, inspiration or methodology; it does not matter, because all you and the audience want is something awesome.

Here is something you might have never heard: you can train yourself to be awesome.

In my opinion, improv is learned behavior. Make-believe and role-play might be instinctual, but improv requires you to work with others, and you have to learn how to do that. Watch kids improvise for five minutes, and you will see how they want to control one another.

You are born with the desire to imitate and with all your natural talents—your voice, your body, and your intellectual aptitude—but to improvise, you must learn how to give up control and cooperate with other humans. I do not think humans are born with this ability. I believe it must be learned.

The problem is that most students don't think their success in improv is based on learning how to cooperate. No, most students think their success in improv is based on how talented or funny they are, as if their success or failure in improv is predetermined and out of their control.

If you are one of these students, let me tell you something—your success is not out of your control. Learning how to improvise takes hard work and practice, and your preconceived notion that you are untalented or not "funny" enough to succeed at improv is your biggest block to success.

What if you disqualified the notion of talent completely? What if your success at improv was based on what you can learn? What if your success in improv was based completely on how well you learned to cooperate with others? What is possible now?

Anything.

When I started doing improv, I had more desire than talent. I was never the kind of improviser who just got up on stage and created magic every time I was in a scene, but I wanted to get better. Honestly, I did not just want to get better—I wanted to be awesome at improv because I loved doing it so much, but I wasn't awesome. I was just okay at it. So, I had to forget the idea that the only way to be a great improviser was to just have the natural talent to do it. If I believed that talent was what made you awesome, then I was never going to be awesome. I had to disqualify the notion of talent completely. I had to base my success at improv on what I could learn. Once I deleted the idea of talent and based my success on what I could learn, I took complete responsibility for my improvement and got a lot better.

I trained myself to be awesome through years of trial and error, because all I had were books and live performances to teach me the way. Through repetition and years of trial and error, I created a bunch of what I call *micro-techniques* to help me be a better improviser. Where another improviser would use their talent, I would develop a micro-technique. I would seem like I was this great improviser who was super-talented, but in reality, I had just trained myself to use a micro-technique. Use a micro-technique enough times and it becomes second nature—you forget you are even using it. Create enough micro-techniques, and you will seem awesome and talented, but really, you will just be well trained.

Here is something else you might have never heard: training is better than talent.

Why?

Because you are in control when it comes to training—especially self-training. You have no control over how talented you are. Talent is something you are born with, like a gift handed down from the gods. Training, on the other hand, is just repetition of step-by-step methods that work for you.

I wanted to live in a world where I was not limited by my natural gifts, so I created step-by-step methods and micro-techniques when my talent was lacking. I don't even see talent anymore; I just see stuff I always knew and stuff I had to learn.

In the first half of the book, I am going to give you the big picture and outline my improv philosophy. Then, in the second half, I will give you my step-by-step process to create awesome scenes and go over every micro-technique I have developed in the past 25 years. I am going to try to keep the philosophy separate from the methodology in the text. That way, you can first see where I am coming from and what I think is important. Then, if you are interested, you can learn how to do it. From time to time, I will go into detail about methodology during the big-picture stuff whenever I think the step-by-step method must be understood in order to get what I am talking about.

These approaches and methods have worked for me, and I have seen them work for hundreds of students. I hope they work for you.

Chapter 2
Stage 1 of the Scenic Structure

The Noodles and the Sauce

Let's take a look at the big picture. You want to get better at doing spontaneous scenes with your partner, so here is a way to look at improv that could help you do that:

The Noodles **and** *the Sauce.*

I know it's difficult to sum up all of improv in a neat little catchphrase, but I am going to do it anyway. Here is my little catchphrase: whenever you do an improv scene you need to give us **the noodles** and **the sauce**. What does that mean? Simply put, the noodles are what you are make-believing and the sauce is how your character feels about it.

Remember, when eating a pasta dinner, you don't eat just noodles and you don't eat just sauce. You need both to have an awesome pasta dinner, and you need both to have an awesome scene.

Let's talk about the noodles for a second. The noodles are whatever you are make-believing. Who you are pretending to be, what you are pretending to do, where you are pretending to be—you know, the make-believe world of the scene. That make-believe is built by figuring out all these specifics, or, as they are often called by improv teachers, the *who, what, where*.

How do you figure out these specifics? By using improv's most fundamental technique: **Yes and...**

Yes and... is the process of taking whatever your partner gives you, agreeing to it (that's the *yes* part), and then adding more to it (that's the *and* part). In a scene, when a player moves or speaks, they are creating specific information about their world. Then that information is *yes and*-ed—it is agreed to and added to. It is this basic back-and-forth between players, this agreeing and adding, that allows for spontaneous collaboration.

At the beginning of a scene, you figure out the specifics of your world by the hard work of offering specific information and *yes and*-ing the heck out of whatever is established until everyone in the scene knows what they are pretending to do. What we are pretending to do is the noodles, and we need that—we need that like crazy.

I mean, think about it—when we go to an Italian restaurant we say, "I'll have the pasta," not, "I'll have the sauce." Noodles are most of what we eat. So, let's just say we need noodles, we need the *who, what, where* stuff; otherwise, no one knows what is going on. But we don't eat just noodles—that would be bland. We want some flavor, so we need some sauce.

Your character's point of view about what is happening in the scene is the sauce. Think about the sauce this way: it is how your character feels about what is happening during the scene. It is how your character feels and why they feel that way. The sauce is what your character wants, why they want it, how they are going to try to get it, and the effect your character doing that stuff has on your scene partner. It's the tasty stuff that leads to fights and laughter and tears in both the real world and the made-up world of your improv scene. The sauce is your character's point of view about what is going on in the scene, and we need that—we need that like crazy.

So, that's the big picture. Every scene needs all the players agreeing to make-believe the same thing (noodles) and every scene needs how your character feels about that agreement (sauce).

Okay, here is the problem with neat little catchphrases that sum up all of improv: If improv is that easy, why do so many scenes fail?

Scenes fail because it is hard to balance the noodles and sauce. We almost always want to add too much of one and not enough of the other, so the ratio is out of whack. There is no magic formula, but here is a way to tell when you need more noodles or more sauce: If you don't know what you are make-believing, you need more noodles, and if you don't know how you feel about it, you need more sauce.

Let's take a closer look.

Most of the time, players don't put enough noodles on the plate. Most of the time when I watch people improvise, I am confused as to what the actors are trying to make-believe. No one ever figures out the specific facts of what the people on stage are pretending to do. For some reason (perhaps because no one ever told them), most improvisers never fully define their world. They never get around to agreeing that they are waiting in line to buy tickets to a U2 concert and it looks like its going to rain or that they are pretending to drive their flunky husband to a job interview because they can't trust him to go alone. That information would be some noodles, and if we can get the specifics out there, then we got a full plate of noodles. If I am in the "waiting in line" scene or the "driving to the job interview" scene, I know all that stuff—I know that I like U2 enough to wait in the rain to buy tickets or I know that I am not competent enough to make it to my own job interview. If I know all that stuff, then I have a real shot at success in this scene.

Why?

Because with the noodles defined and out there, I know how to pretend, how to behave, and how to make-believe that I am in that line or in that car. With that much agreement and make-believe going on, I am going to start to feel something based on the scene rather than the anxiety of doing improv. I am going to discover a strong point of view inside the make-believe scene, and when that happens, I can yell, scream, or laugh at the other person in the scene if I want. I can pour on the sauce, because there are enough noodles, or context, to support the tension. With everyone in the room (and I mean everyone—me, my scene partner, and the audience) on the same page and understanding what we are asking everyone to believe in (the noodles), we can focus completely on point of view (the sauce). With the agreement completely established, you can just feel the way you feel in the scene and commit to heightening that feeling.

Without the noodles, no one cares about the sauce. If the world of the scene is undefined, then the audience won't care about the character's point of view. That is what this book is going to teach you: how to create scenes that the audience will care about. Read that sentence again. I did not say anything about being funny. This book will not make you funny. This book can help you do scenes that people care about. Why will the people watching care about your scenes? Because they will understand what they are being asked to believe in. Why will they understand? Because they will get some noodles first. You will learn to establish scenes by building the world. You will learn to start with the noodles. Then you will learn to add the sauce—the flavor, or your character's point of view. If you give the audience the noodles and the sauce, they will care about your scene. And if they care, they will laugh and cry and give a heck about what happens to your character. If the audience cares about your character, they will watch your improv scenes for the same reason they watch movies, television shows, and plays—to empathize with the characters and see what happens. If that kind of improv sounds awesome to you, let's get to work.

Say Yes to Saying Yes

In an improv scene, literally anything can happen. You can create any possible world when you do a scene. But, even though anything can happen, you need to figure out the specifics of your "anything" early on. The anything sure is exciting. It is the potential energy of your scene, but you can't play with anything—you have to play with something, and that something needs to be specific. You could start with any specific, like "I am on a boat" or "I am a mother" or "I am afraid of bees." There are no good or bad specifics; we just need them, whatever they are.

Why do you need to define the specifics of the scene early on?

So the world of the scene will become real for you. Specifics help create reality. They are the building blocks of the world of the scene that you can believe in.

For example, if a player starts a scene with this line:

> "I love being on your boat, Ron."

That is something specific that both players can grab a hold of and believe in. Being on a boat is something we can make real for ourselves, and if these characters can really be on that boat for a moment and deal with all the real stuff that is there—the wind, the sun, the rocking of the boat—then something meaningful could happen between them. Because they won't be improvisers on stage anymore—they will be characters on a boat.

Making specific choices at the top of your scene is one of your most important obligations as an improviser. In fact, I believe it is your second most important job at the top of a scene. Your most important job at the top of a scene is to say *yes* to the specific stuff your partner creates.

Why is it more important to say *yes* to your partner's ideas than your own?

Because you are not in control of your partner, and dealing with what they give you keeps you spontaneous. It keeps you in a situation where you can't know what is going to happen next. In a state where nobody is in charge, you are forced to rely on each other to succeed, and everything could fall apart at any moment.

What keeps any scene from falling apart and dissolving into chaos? The cooperation among the players.

We cooperate by saying yes to the other guy's idea. That is what keeps any scene from falling apart—agreeing to everything that has been established. That means saying yes to the other guy. For me, that is the only qualitative measurement for improv: how good the group is at saying yes to each other's ideas—how well they cooperate.

How do you say *yes* to the specifics your partner creates?

Focus completely on your partner when they are contributing something to the scene. This might sound like a simple solution, but most people learning how to improvise are obsessed with themselves. They are self-conscious. They are consumed with how well they are doing and are nearly blind to what their partner is creating. Practice focusing completely on the other person, and see what you can harvest from what they do and say. If you actively focus on the other while they contribute stuff in the scene, you will respond in a way that builds upon what has already been established.

So, say *yes* to saying *yes*.

Say *yes* to specifics given to you by your partner. Say *yes* to your own ideas and feelings—ideas and feelings that are collaborative and based on building together with your partner.

The Three Stages of a Scene

Improv scenes have a structure—a beginning, a middle, and an end, so to speak—just like a movie. In the beginning of a movie, the filmmaker has to set the scene and introduce the characters. We want to know where this film is taking place, so filmmakers give us this information by showing us where the characters live and work. They take us inside the characters' world. In the beginning of a movie, we also want to know who the movie is about, so filmmakers give us this information by showing us the characters doing stuff—stuff that communicates what kind of person the character is. If we see a character chopping wood, we assume they are tough and outdoorsy. If we see a character hugging their kid when they pick them up from school, we figure they are nurturing and parental.

In the beginning of any narrative—a movie, a book, or an improv scene—the storyteller is responsible for establishing the world the narrative inhabits. In improvisation, you are the storyteller, so it's your responsibility to establish the world.

That is the first job for any improviser starting a scene: Figure out and establish the world of the scene. I call this beginning part of the scene—where improvisers are figuring out and establishing their world—the noodles, or stage one of the scenic structure. Once you complete the work that stage one requires, you can move on to the next stage in the structure, but I am getting ahead of myself.

Here is a way to structure every scene you will ever do that can help you build something specific and meaningful for your character:

Improv scenes have three distinct stages, and each stage has a different job it does for the scene. You can train yourself to know what stage of the scene you're in and master the skills needed to do the work that each stage demands. Think of the three stages this way: the noodles, the sauce, and the spice.

THE THREE STAGES OF AN IMPROV SCENE

Stage One
The Noodles

Building the Agreement

The specific stuff you and your partner(s) do and agree to in order to establish what you are make-believing.

Stage Two
The Sauce

*Exploration of Point of View
to Discover the Primary
Emotional Drive*

The characters explore their Point of View about their world, which includes other characters, the environment, and the dramatic situation. This exploration leads characters to the discovery of their Primary Emotional Drive or what they care the most about.

Stage Three
The Spice

Heightening

The specific stuff you and your partner(s) do to make everyone feel the way they feel more, as well as the specific stuff everyone in the scene does to increase the stakes of the given circumstances.

Really, every time I step out to do a scene, the first thing I am thinking is "What am I agreeing to?" I might initiate with something specific, or try to figure out what I am being given by my partner, but my underlying thought is "What am I saying *yes* to?" I am actively and aggressively searching for something to say *yes* to and will not be satisfied until I harvest something to *yes* from what is going on around me.

After I build the agreement with my partner and know the world I am playing in, then I move on to "How do I feel about it?" and "How does my partner feel about it?" Once I figure out my point of view and my partner's point of view, I explore those feelings until I discover what feeling is the strongest and what my character cares about in this world. This feeling that is the strongest is my Primary Emotional Drive.

Once my partner and I discover our Primary Emotional Drives, I think, "How can I make myself and my partner feel that way—more?"

I answer the "What am I agreeing to?" question before I move on to the "How do I feel about it?" question. This way, I am basing my feelings on the specifics of the scenic agreement. Then, after I answer the "How do my partner and I feel in the scene?" question, I move on to the "How can I make both of us feel that way—more?" question. Remember, it is the "What am I agreeing to?" question that is the most important. Everything is based on answering that fundamental question.

This approach to scene work can make everything so much easier, because if everyone in the scene is trained to begin scenes by building the make-believe world together, then they will get to something specific—fast. Starting with building the scenic agreement is not what improvisers usually do; it is not natural to walk into the void of an empty stage and start cooperating. That void scares us, so our fight-or-flight instincts kick in and we panic. That panic is real for us, and we put that feeling into the scene. Because of this, inexperienced players usually start with a negative point of view and go directly to heightening that negativity, without building a scenic agreement first. This negative point of view is unearned. These negative feelings are not authentic to the scene; they are authentic to the improviser. They are not character feelings based on the make-believe world. The negativity getting forced on to the scene is based on the real world, where you are in a theatre or rehearsal space or bar, doing a scene in front of people you want to impress with your talent. Your character does not feel anxiety about the people watching him/her thinking he/she is talented. Your character feels stuff based on their reality, without giving the slightest thought as to whether other people will find it funny or not.

During stage one of the scene, you don't even know what you're make-believing yet. You need to know what your world is before you know how you feel about it so you can discover your character's Primary Emotional Drive as a product of the scenic agreement.

Once the basic anxiety of doing improv wears off (and this can take years for some people), starting with character point of view can work. Just remember, it's character point of view—not actor point of view. You need to be honest with yourself about this; ask yourself, "Am I starting most scenes with a negative point of view because of what is happening between the characters in the make-believe world, or am I just projecting my own personal anxiety on to the scene?" If you are forcing your anxiety on to the scene, perhaps you're just not comfortable making stuff up yet. Stick with it, and give yourself some time. The longer you improvise, the more comfortable you will become.

What I encourage is following the three stages in order and doing the work that each stage demands. If I follow the stages in order, I first build something specific and meaningful with my partner that I can believe in. Next, I figure out how this specific world makes my partner and I feel. Then, I heighten my partner's feelings and allow myself to be heightened.

Building a Scene Is Like Flying a Plane

Here is another metaphor that may help convince you of the importance of following the three stages of a scene in order:

Building a scene is like flying a plane.

I know we are working on this whole "the agreement is the noodles and the exploration of point of view to discover Primary Emotional Drive is the sauce" thing. And now, with stage three—heightening—I have thrown a third ingredient into the "scene as food" metaphor—heightening is spice. Even with this whole food metaphor cooking, I am going to use another analogy to help illustrate the importance of the three stages happening in sequence.

Building a scene is like flying a plane.

When you fly a plane, there are three distinct stages: takeoff, flying, and landing. Each stage of flight is different. Each stage requires the pilots to focus on different information and rely on different skills. When a plane is rolling down the runway, if you try to take off too early, the plane is never going to get off the ground and might just crash and burn. During takeoff, you have to pay attention to specific details—tons of details, like speed, wind, and runway length. You have to meticulously figure out and establish how you are going to get the plane off the ground. Missing a small piece of information can really botch a takeoff, and you should know that most crashes happen during takeoff. Each phase of flight requires you to focus on the job that stage needs to get done. While taking off, you have to focus on taking off. Focusing on later stages, like flying or landing, will only make it harder to actually get the plane off the ground.

Once the plane is in the air, you can stop taking off and just fly in whatever direction the plane is headed.

In terms of scenic structure, the takeoff is stage one: building the agreement. The details are very important, and if you miss a piece of information, the scene could crash. If you push point of view too much at the top of a scene, before everyone knows what is going on, it is like trying to take off before the plane has enough speed. So, during the takeoff of your scene, focus on details and specifics, provide information, and define the make-believe world. Figure out what kind of plane you are in before you try to get it off the ground.

Pilots need to recognize what stage of flight they are in so they know what job to focus on. They need to recognize that they are in the takeoff phase of flight so they can focus on taking off, and the same is true for improvisers doing scene work.

In a scene, do each job completely and know your obligations. You will start to learn how it feels to be in each stage, and you will begin developing specific skills to help you do your job better.

Chapter 3
The Five Scenic Elements: CREPP

Every scene needs to start with stage one: building the agreement (or the noodles) with the improvisers doing specific stuff with their bodies and voices to establish the make-believe world. And stage one isn't complete until everyone is on the same page and knows what they are make-believing. So, let's take a closer look at stage one/the noodles and what I call the *five scenic elements*.

What exactly are you creating during stage one, when you step out on stage and do something specific with your body and voice?

If you start a scene by sitting in a chair and typing, what have you created? If you pace back and forth and wring your hands, what specific stuff have you created for the scene? Literally, everything you and your partner do together creates something scenic, but what?

What are we creating in the beginning of a scene, during stage one?

Let's take a look.

Say you step out into the void of the stage, grab an imaginary glass of wine, and say to your partner, "John, this is a wonderful going-away party." Yay, you did it. You did something specific with your body—you grabbed a wine glass, not a bottle of beer or a mug of coffee, but a wine glass. You also did something specific with your voice, you named your scene partner, and told us where you are: a going-away party. You even told us how you feel about it: wonderful. These specifics, coupled with the way you said your line and how you moved as you said it, start to define the world of the scene. Your scene is in stage one; you have given us some noodles and started the process of creating specifics to build the scenic agreement. You did something with your body and voice to put some stuff out into the universe, and that stuff needs to be *yes and*-ed until everyone knows what is going on.

But when you do something specific, like sitting in a chair and typing or grabbing a glass of wine, what stuff is being put out into the universe? What exactly are we creating when we do something specific to start an improv scene? And after my partner makes an offer, what exactly am I *yes and*-ing? What are we agreeing to, and what kind of stuff should we add? Each piece of information you are putting out there establishes something real in the world of the scene, but what? What are the fundamental building blocks of a scene?

All matter, in its most basic form, is made up of elements. Like water, for instance—if you break water down into its smallest parts, you will find it is not water, but hydrogen and oxygen—two elements that are nothing like water. These two elements bond together to form water. Improv can be looked at in the same way. If you break a scene down into its most basic parts, you will find five elements, or what I call *CREPP*. The five elements (in no particular order) are the following:

Character
Relationship
Environment
Point of view
Point of attack

Improv scenes are made of these five elements. In fact, any scene, improvised or scripted, that achieves the goal of getting the audience to care is made of these five elements. These five scenic elements are just things you need to know in order to connect with the story being told during the scene.

If you establish these five elements every time you create a scene, you and your audience will feel connected to the character's world. Why? Because you will have built the world of the scene enough for the actors and audience to start believing in it. It is not just about you believing in the world of the scene—we are trying to get everyone on the same page, including the audience. By establishing the five scenic elements, you trigger an automatic, learned response that humans have to narrative. These five scenic elements are not just used to create improv scenes—they are the building blocks of any narrative, no matter how it is presented.

And humans have an automatic, conditioned response to narrative. As Donald Polkinghorne says in his book *Narrative Knowing and the Human Sciences*, narrative is "the primary form by which human experience is made meaningful."

That is what people are doing when they watch your improv scenes—looking for meaning. They are just trying to figure out how what you are doing relates to their lives. At this point, you may be thinking, "Wow, I thought they just came to have a good time—this is getting kind of heavy."

No worries, because I've got some good news for you. Good news part one: if you establish the five elements, they will automatically relate your scene to their lives. They will automatically assign narrative meaning to what you are doing in the scene. If you establish the five scenic elements, they will form emotional bonds with your character and begin to fashion your behavior in the scene into a story. They will assign cause and effect to what they are watching and start to care about what is happening to your character, as long as the five scenic elements are defined or implied. It is just what humans naturally do.

And here's good news part two: anything you do—any sound you utter, any movement your body makes, literally anything you do on stage—creates one or more of the five scenic elements. You may not know you are creating them, but you are. When you make-believe, you automatically create these scenic elements. The problem is that most improvisers don't even know these scenic elements exist and, therefore, place no conscious effort in creating them. For me, establishing the five scenic elements has become automatic. But I did not start out that way. I had to train myself to do it.

Here's how I did it.

First, I made establishing scenic elements a conscious process. I focused on defining the elements whenever I did scenes. I learned that when you clearly define a single element, other elements are automatically defined. I discovered that physicality helps define character and that a strong character usually knew where they were, so I could use character to discover environment.

I began isolating elements when I started scenes, just like an athlete will isolate a muscle when they are lifting weights at the gym. Focusing on a single element and forcing myself to initiate a scene by establishing that element first strengthened my ability to use them to create the world of the scene. After a while (and lots of practice isolating elements), I could consciously establish any element at any time during a scene.

Breaking a scene down into its parts helped me understand how scenes are made. I truly started seeing these elements as the building blocks for creating scenes. For me, recognizing the smaller pieces that you assemble to make the bigger thing helped tremendously.

It has helped me become a better improviser to think about creating the parts of a scene, rather than making the whole thing. In fact, I don't know how to "make an improv scene" any more than a carpenter knows how to "make a house." A carpenter knows how to build a wall and a floor and a doorframe, and eventually, after they build all these smaller things, they have a house. And I know how to build an agreement, one element at a time, and after my partner and I have established all five elements, we have a scene.

So, basically, I am saying in order to make a house or a pasta dinner or an improv scene, you have to break the thing you are trying to make down into its parts and make the parts instead of the whole thing. As you put the parts together, the whole starts to take shape and tells us what it wants to be. Like I said before, clearly define one scenic element and the rest of the scene comes along for the ride. Let's look at each element, one at a time:

Character
(who you are in the scene)

Character is created by what you do and how you do it, in the context of the world of the scene.

Character is something you do. It is active. We know someone is the kind of person they are by observing their behavior. We watch what they do, how they do it, and in what context they do it. What a character does and how they do it are equally important factors in telling us the kind of person we are watching.

Character is not a title like a fireman but a series of behaviors and actions that have a defined "how" in the context of the world of the scene. Sure, you can be a fireman, but what kind of fireman are you?

Let's say we see a character sitting at his desk in a fire station when a call comes in about a fire. This character responds by taking his sweet time putting on his fireman boots and coat. While the other firemen are getting ready as fast as they can to fight the fire, he stops by the mirror to check his hair. Before sliding down the pole to the fire truck, he checks his phone to see if he has any messages.

He is not the label of "fireman," but the sum of what he does and how he does it in the context of the world of the scene. By the time he gets on that fire truck, his actions, in context, have told us everything we need to know to understand what kind of person this guy is.

Relationship
(how the characters are connected to each other and the effect those connections have on their behavior)

Relationship is created by establishing a set of connections between the characters.

I call these connections *Relationship Components*. These connections, or Relationship Components, lead to a cause-and-effect pattern of behavior between the characters. This cause and effect is repeated and heightened by the characters. The repetition and heightening of cause and effect creates the *Dynamic*.

If there is a holy grail in improv, it is the idea that every scene is "about the relationship," but what does that mean? What is relationship in terms of improv scene work? Using a label like "mother/daughter" does not cut it, just like the label "fireman" does not cut it to define character. Don't get me wrong—I think defining the two characters as mother and daughter is a great thing to do; I just don't think that information gets you all the way to relationship. We need more information to determine what kind of "mother/daughter" we have on our hands.

Who the characters are to each other is a living, breathing thing, just like in real life. Try to describe who you and your mother "are to each other" with a simple title—you can't. You have spent your life becoming the way you are with each other; it is more nuanced than the label "mother/daughter."

But you can break down all the ways in which you are connected to your mother into what I call Relationship Components. These Relationship Components are history, emotion, status, physicality, space, and sensuality. Some of the components are static and do not change, like history, while some are constantly changing, like status. So, in improv, relationship is the process of defining a set of Relationship Components. These connections create a cause and effect between the characters inside the context of the world of the scene. This cause and effect between characters is repeated and heightened and yields the Dynamic.

When you see a really awesome scene where the characters are super-connected and hanging on each other's every word, one of those scenes that was both funny and real, where the players missed nothing and you would have watched it for hours, what you are watching is the Dynamic between the characters (Relationship Components and the Dynamic are discussed in chapter 18).

Environment
(where the scene takes place)

The environment of the scene is everything that is there—anything you can touch, see, hear, taste, and smell.

We experience our real-life environment with all five of our senses. We feel the texture of the fabric of the couch on the back of our legs. We see the sunlight coming through our bedroom window. We hear the dripping water in the back of the cave. We taste the stale ribbon candy in grandma's parlor. We smell the hamburgers on the grill in the backyard. And we also want to experience our make-believe environment with all five of our senses. Visualizing our imaginary world is the first step, but we can't stop there. We need to invite all the senses to the imagination party. We need to touch, see, hear, taste, and smell our imaginary world so it can become real for our character and real for our audience.

Sure, you can define the environment of the scene by saying, "Wow, this is a big barn." But you can also play with all the stuff that is there and see, hear, taste, and smell the barn, too.

We want the make-believe setting for the scene to be as detailed as the real world, so declaring, "Wow, this is a big barn," is a good start but just the beginning of the work that needs to be done. If you touch, see, hear, taste, and smell your world, the audience will, too.

If you don't, they won't.

Point of View
(how your character thinks and feels about the people, places, and things in the world of the scene)

Point of view is created by your character's imagined past, as well as responding to what is happening in the "here and now" of the scene. During a scene, characters will discover a point of view that becomes more and more intense over time. I call this point of view that gets more intense over time the *Primary Emotional Drive*.

Look around the room you are in right now. You will have a point of view about almost every thing you see. You will know how you feel about each object and person, and you will know why you feel that way. You will even have a feeling about the room you are in. You won't have to figure out how you feel about these people, places, and things. You will have perfect knowledge of your point of view and why you feel that way. You will know that these feelings are right for you, and you will treat each of these people, places, and things based on your point of view, coupled with your reason for why you feel that way.

You won't have to work or think at all to figure out any of these feelings about all this stuff around you. Your rich, detailed, and emotional point of view will be based on your previous experiences with all this stuff.

This rich and detailed relationship to our surroundings is what we are trying to make-believe in improv scenes. We can make-believe our character's point of view during scene work in the same way we believe it in the real world. We feel the way we feel about the stuff in our lives because of our past experience with that stuff. We feel the way we feel about the people in our lives because of how they treated us in the past and how they are treating us in the present. This is the exact way we can encounter our point of view in make-believe scene work.

If we can imagine our character's past, we can play their present.

We want our character's point of view in scene work to be rooted in an imagined history, but we also want it to be responsive to what is happening among the characters, here and now. We want our characters to discover point of view by being in the moment. Being in the moment allows our characters to discover point of view by being altered by our scene partner.

At some point during the scene, our character will spontaneously discover a point of view that becomes more and more intense over time. As this point of view grows in intensity, it begins to motivate the character's behavior. The character will do stuff because of this point of view. I call this intensifying point of view that motivates behavior the character's Primary Emotional Drive.

The discovery of your character's Primary Emotional Drive is stage two of your scene—it is the sauce. And it is this Primary Emotional Drive that is going to be heightened during the rest of the scene—heightened by you and heightened by your scene partner (point of view and Primary Emotional Drive are discussed in depth in chapter 6).

Point of Attack
(when in the story the scene takes place)

Where you are picking up the story at the start of the scene.

Every scene creates a story. The point of attack is when, in the broader timeline of the story, the action of the scene starts. Scenes in movies, plays, and television shows pick up the narrative late in the action of the story. They pick up the action after the characters have known each other for years, sometimes since birth. When we dramatize stories, we cut to the moments that are either most typical or most dramatic for the characters. Writers fast-forward their stories to scenes containing characters with shared history, dealing with stuff they care deeply about. When they do this, they are manipulating point of attack to get to the interesting stuff. Improvisers can do the same by moving the point of attack for their scenes to events in the story's timeline that are full of tension.

You can either discover where in the story you are or consciously choose that the scene takes place "the night before your character gets married." It does not matter if you *yes and* your way to your point of attack or just declare when in your story's timeline you want to be—all that matters is that you get that information into the scene so you can play with it.

The later the point of attack is in the narrative, the closer your scene is to the climax of the story. As you get closer to the climax of the story, you build more tension in the scene and more history between the characters, which is more fun to play.

I look at the five scenic elements as a checklist for the strength of a scene. If all five elements are defined and agreed to, then the scene has a real shot at success. The elements are just what you and the audience need to be defined in order to believe in the world of the scene. We unconsciously create scenic elements when we make-believe. If you touch an imagined doorknob, you are adding the element of environment. If you tell your scene partner, "Thanks for the ride home," you have established point of attack. Anything you do can be plugged into the five elements. The five basic building blocks are what you create when you improvise. As you and your partner create specific stuff with what you do and say, it is important to recognize what element is being added to the scene. Once an element is established, it needs to be agreed to so it can become real in the world of the scene.

You also need to know what elements are lacking in your scene. Most of the time if a scene fails to make the audience care, it is because one (or more) of the elements was not defined. Remember there is no right or wrong choice when it comes to defining a scenic element. You can't have a "wrong" environment for a scene, so just go ahead and define the elements of your scene. Then play in your world.

Chapter 4
The Join

A Philosophy: You + Me = We

Before we move on to stage two (the sauce) and three (the spice) of the scenic structure, I want to talk about a little something I call *the Join*.

If there is one radical idea in this book, one method that I have created that you will not be taught anywhere else that will completely change the way you do improv, it is the Join. The Join is an improv philosophy and a step-by-step method to start a scene.

In this chapter, I am going to talk about the philosophy of the Join. I might lose a few of you here, because I am about to get a little motivational speaker-ish, but I do think this is important, so try to bear with me.

The Join, as a philosophy, is an approach to scene work that gets the improv actor to put the focus on *we* instead of *me* (the self). The philosophy of the Join is, literally, to train your brain to think, "We are on a boat," instead of "I am on a boat," when you start a scene. The Join assumes a connection between the characters and asks you to include your partner in your idea or be included in their idea. The Join takes focus off the self (me) and places it on partnership (we). You are not improvising alone; you have a partner, so you might as well perceive yourself as joined with them. You are anyway—you are doing a scene together.

You are part of the *we*, and your partner is part of the *we*, but the *we* is bigger than both of you.

The team is more important than the player. The scene is more important than the actor. The *we* is more important than you and me.

My priority when I improvise is working with my partner and collaborating with my team—you know, good old-fashioned teamwork. And by doing this collaboration, I participate in creating something bigger and more important than just myself. That is what I mean by "you + me = we." For me, creating a *we* is the goal. Every time I do a scene, I am trying to answer the question "What are we agreeing to?" When I improvise, I see my partner and myself connected as a *we*. In order to do that, I have to join with my partner, both in the way I think about them and with my body.

When I improvise, I am not alone. I am connected to my partner, and they are connected to me. We belong to each other. We are creating something together, so it is important that we perceive ourselves as joined. I don't care if this sounds strange or if the idea of "belonging" to your partner puts you way out of your comfort zone; trust me, this "you + me = we" connectedness is the philosophy of the Join.

Okay, so you can tell I am really into the Join as a philosophy, but what is the step-by-step method and how do you do it? Turn the page.

A Step-by-Step Method

The Join is a philosophy, but it is also a specific way to create the top of a scene, whether you come in with an idea or are starting with nothing. The Join works in every situation, long form or short form, two-person scenes or group scenes—it does not matter. You can always use the Join at the top of the scene to create a *we* and get everyone on the same page.

Starting a scene with a join defines something specific about how the characters are connected—immediately. The players do this by using their bodies before they speak. The Join is the simple act of going out there and being with your partner by utilizing your body at the top of the scene.

At Theatre 99, where I teach and perform, students learn the Join during their first class and every scene starts with a join.

Let's take a look at the basic Join drill.

Note to the reader: The second half of this book is devoted to step-by-step methods and exercises; however, I just think that the Join is too important to wait. If we are figuring out and establishing what we are make-believing during stage one of the scenic structure, then the Join is fundamental.

THE JOIN DRILL: ROUND ONE
(ABSTRACT MOVEMENT)

Note: Round one of the Join drill is not a scenic exercise—it is just a way to get players used to joining with their bodies before they speak. Here it is.

Step 1: Everyone stands in a circle.

Step 2: One person steps into the circle and begins doing an abstract movement. (I call this person *the beginner*.)

Step 3: With the beginner moving in the center of the circle, prompt another player to step into the circle and join the movement. (I call this person *the joiner*.)

Step 4: The two players in the circle move together for a few moments, then you call scene. The two players return to the edge of the circle.

Step 5: Repeat steps 1–4 until everyone has gone.

When I introduce a group to the Join drill for the first time, I always have them start with abstract movement.
Why?
Because I want the players to learn that the Join is about support, and when you support someone, you don't wait to figure out what they are doing. You just go out there to be with your partner, before you even understand what they are doing. If you wait to know what is going on before you support, then you are not supporting—you are focusing on yourself instead of focusing on the *we*.
So, when I introduce the Join drill, I require the beginner to step into the circle and do an abstract movement. This gets the group to do this very important thing. It forces everyone to join something they cannot understand—somebody else's crazy abstract movement—and if they can do that, then they can pretty much

join anything.

Here are some other things you need to know in order to teach your group round one of the Join drill:

Before you start:

Give examples of what abstract movement looks like. Regular humans don't have any experience moving in an abstract way. Why would they? I define abstract and concrete movement as follows: if the player knows what their movement represents, then it is concrete. If they don't, then it is abstract.

During step 2:

When the beginner steps into the circle and establishes their abstract movement, encourage him or her to continue doing it—push them to repeat the movement and keep it abstract.

During step 3:

When the joiner enters the circle, tell them they can join in any way they want, with concrete or abstract movement.

During step 4:

You will have two people moving inside the circle. Their movement might still be completely abstract. Even though the players have joined, they might not have a clue what they are doing or the joiner might have made some sense out of the beginner's abstract movement by how they joined.

Either way is fine. Now let's take a look at how players are joining. After you get your group to do the abstract Join drill for a while, the way players are joining will start to look similar. That is because, for beginners, there are three basic ways to join. Here they are.

THE THREE BASIC WAYS TO JOIN

1. More of the Same

Example: Someone steps out and does an abstract movement like waving their arms around. Then someone else in the circle thinks, "Hey, she is waving her arms around. I can do that." Then that person steps out and starts waving their arms around. Now we have two people, in the middle of the circle, waving their arms around. The joiner saw what was happening and added more of the same.

2. Complete the Picture

Example: Someone steps out and does an abstract movement like grabbing their stomach with their mouth wide open. Then someone else in the circle thinks, "Hey, that guy looks like he is laughing; I'll go out there and tickle him." Then that person steps out and starts tickling the beginner. The joiner saw the picture of someone tickling the beginner in his/her brain and stepped out to complete that picture.

3. Contact

Example: Someone steps out and does an abstract movement like hopping on one foot. Then someone else in the circle thinks, "Hey, that guy is hopping on one foot; I'll go stand behind him and put my hands on his shoulders." Then that person steps out, stands behind the beginner, and puts his hands on the beginner's shoulders. The joiner has made physical contact with the beginner.

When I introduce a group to the Join for the first time, I never tell them these three basic ways to join. I always make them figure it out for themselves by doing the exercise. For me, the purpose of the Join drill is for the players to discover these three types of joins without any help from me.

Why? Because it helps the players think of themselves as part of a *we*. If they are trying to figure out how to join their partner, then they are trying to connect, and that is half the battle. Also, forcing players to join without telling them how allows them to learn by doing. When players discover how to do something instead of being told what to do, it sticks better. So, I don't tell them how to do it. I just watch them try, and when they do a join, I ask the group how the players did it. I get the group to tell me how the players joined. After the group discovers each type of join, I will describe it in a little more detail.

After the group gets comfortable with the act of joining abstract movement, I have them try starting the Join drill with concrete movement.

THE JOIN DRILL: ROUND TWO (CONCRETE)

Step 1: Everyone stands in a circle.

Step 2: The beginner steps into the circle and starts doing a concrete movement.

Step 3: The joiner steps in and joins the beginner's concrete movement.

Step 4: The two players in the circle move together for a few moments, then you call scene. The two players return to the edge of the circle.

Step 5: Repeat steps 1–4 until everyone has gone.

Yep, it is the same exercise as round one, except now players begin and join with concrete movement. These concrete joins will look just like the tops of scenes. Just by the act of joining each other physically, the players will create connections with each other—spontaneously.

It is important to note that the Join is not an entrance; we are not watching a scene where a character is alone and then another character enters the same space. We are watching the pre-scene, where we see the creative process at work. The Join is not the scene, but the transformation into the scene.

You can use these three basic ways to join—more of the same, complete the picture, and contact—regardless of what your partner gives you. It does not matter if your partner starts with something abstract or concrete, because the three basic joins work in any situation, even if you have no idea what your partner is doing.

Let's take a look at three examples of basic joins where the beginner starts with concrete movement.

THE THREE BASIC JOINS

1. More of the Same

Example: Someone steps out and starts doing the Twist. Then someone else in the circle thinks, "Hey, she is doing the Twist. I can do the Twist." Then that person steps out and starts doing the Twist. Now we have two people in the circle doing the Twist. The joiner saw what was happening and added more of the same.

2. Complete the Picture

Example: Someone steps out and starts swinging a baseball bat. Then someone else in the circle thinks, "Hey, that guy is swinging a baseball bat; I'll go out there and pitch him the ball." Then that person steps out and starts pitching the ball to the beginner. The joiner saw the picture of the beginner playing baseball in his/her brain and then stepped out and completed that picture.

3. Contact

Example: Someone steps out and starts the pantomime of washing dishes. Then someone else in the circle thinks, "Hey, that guy is washing dishes; I'll go stand behind him and put my hands on his shoulders." Then that person steps out, stands behind the beginner, and puts his hands on his/her shoulders. The joiner has made physical contact with the beginner.

When I teach this exercise, I talk about what changes when the beginner is joined. I ask the group after every join if something scenic was created. They usually say *yes* because they can see the potential for interaction between the characters after each join. This is also true in the three examples above—when the beginner was joined, something scenic started to happen.

Okay, you have your team doing concrete joins to start scenes. What does that give you? Why do I think this join thing is such a big deal?

Because the Join spontaneously defines scenic elements right off the bat, and you know by now how important I think scenic elements are when it comes to building a scene. If you do a join to start a scene, you are just that much further ahead of the game because you and your partner are already on the same page and agreeing with each other. You are already creating the world of the scene with your bodies.

Let's look at the three examples of concrete joins I've already used.

1. More of the Same

Example: In this join, we have two people dancing the Twist. All we have to do is watch the way they dance and we will know if they are at a 1950s sock hop or a present-day dance club. And what's really awesome is that the players might not even know until they start dancing together. They may just discover where they are and what they are doing by relating to each other physically, before they even speak.

2. Complete the Picture

Example: In this join, we have one person swinging a bat and another person pitching a ball. These characters have already established a cause-and-effect relationship. They are well on their way to discovering the Dynamic between the characters. I already care about their world because I see them as joined, as a *we*. Honestly, these characters could be in any environment and I would watch to find out what happens.

3. Contact

Example: In this join, we have one character embracing another while they wash dishes. All either of these characters have to do is take a deep breath and sigh, then—bang—we have lovers in the kitchen who are trying to make up after a fight. All five elements have either been established or suggested, and no one has even spoken yet.

How much fun is it going to be to play this scene, with all the hard work done before the first line of dialogue? A lot of fun, because the make-believe has already begun. These players are not improvisers trying to be funny. They are characters believing in their world and dealing with their reality.

So, I do joins to start scenes, every time. It connects you to your partner before you even speak. It works if you have a specific scenic idea or not. It defines scenic elements spontaneously and immediately. It gets individuals to see themselves as part of a group and start cooperating with their partners—and isn't that what improv is all about?

Chapter 5
The Click

So far in this book, I have been selling you the idea of making conscious choices to start scenes. I have been preaching a way to improvise that requires you to think your way into a scene—literally, to figure out what you are make-believing. To think, "We are on a boat," or "We are brother and sister," when you start a scene. To consciously choose what you add to a scene, and to even be able to categorize the type of information you contribute into what I call *scenic elements*. The whole noodles and sauce thing asks you to be aware of whether or not you have entered into a scenic agreement with your partner. But honestly, checking off the list of scenic elements at the top of a scene is not all that much fun. It is certainly not why I love improv or why I keep doing it.

I have the most fun when I lose myself in a scene. When I stop consciously thinking about what to do next. When my character takes over, and they are the one making the decisions.

That's what I am working for in a scene—to have the make-believe take over. I am trying to create the moment when my brain switches from the conscious thought of "What is our scenic agreement" to the unconscious thought of my character's point of view. This switch from the conscious to the unconscious happens when I drop into the world of the scene, and I am no longer thinking as an improviser but as a character. The term *drop in* is how I describe my conscious choice to suspend my disbelief and treat this make-believe world as real. When I drop in, my improviser brain switches to autopilot and my behavior becomes automatic and unconscious as my character starts to do and say stuff in their world.

I have a little name for this mental switch. I call it *the Click*. The Click is an actual sensation you can feel when your mind switches from conscious thought to automatic/unconscious thought, and the Click feels good.

So if the Click feels good, why start scenes with all that not-so-fun conscious thought about scenic elements? Why wouldn't we just start with the Click?

Why? Because that good feeling we get when the Click happens is not free. We have to work for the Click. In other words, we have to pay for the fun.

We have to do a lot of thinking at the top of the scene because nothing is defined for us in improvisation. We have to choose and create our world and figure out a bunch of stuff with our partner, but then we get to have a bunch of fun and just play.

That's what I have trained myself to do—to consciously create my make-believe world by choosing and agreeing to scenic elements. Then I consciously drop into that world and switch from improviser mind to character mind—that's the Click. I get in character and I get in the moment. In this state of being, I truly see the world through my character's eyes and just do whatever my character wants to do.

This is the fun part.

It is thrilling to drop into the scene and ride the roller coaster of my character's emotions as they respond to their scene partner. It's fun to lose yourself and take the ride, but you have to pay for the fun.

That is my approach—pay for the fun by building the make-believe world one scenic element at a time. As you improvise, you keep an awareness of the scenic elements you create. You keep creating these elements until the scene feels real. That's why you train your brain to think in scenic elements, not as a rule or to be a good improviser, but because if you commit to defining and agreeing to scenic elements, sooner or later the scene will become real for you. It is this reality you have created with your partner that you drop into and in which you must believe.

My approach uses a conscious process of creating scenic elements as a pathway to encountering unconscious character thoughts. Yep, I am suggesting that you use thinking as a way to stop thinking.

I use my brain to find the scene so my character can get lost in it. When this truly happens, I am not myself for a few minutes—I am the character and I am completely free.

How to Create the Click by Using "The Method"

So, at the top of a scene, I am completely focused on establishing scenic elements as a way to form an agreement with my partner. But I am only doing this to create something I can drop into. Establishing scenic elements is not the goal; the goal is to create something with my partner in which I can believe. The moment the scene becomes real for me and I see the world through my character's eyes is what I call *the Click*.

Okay, so how do you do this? How do you make the scene real and see the world through your character's eyes?

First, you have to make establishing scenic elements automatic. Automaticity is the ability to do something without thinking about every little step involved, like when you drive your car on a long road trip. When you drive hundreds of miles, there are whole stretches of the trip where you are not aware that you are driving. While you drive, you might be talking to the person beside you or listening to music or a *This American Life* podcast, but at some point, you zone out, and the driving becomes automatic. This automaticity comes from years of repetition and practice. You have to make establishing scenic elements as automatic as driving your car on long road trips. You have to train yourself to establish scenic elements without even thinking about it.

And remember, to establish a scenic element, you have to believe in the element. It is not enough to just verbally mention where you are in the scene. For example, if you start a scene by saying, "It sure is hot in this barn," as a way to establish environment, remember you have not established environment until you believe that you are there—until the barn becomes real to you. Just saying you are in a hot barn does not make it real.

So, here we are again—improv is acting and acting is believing. So, how do you create belief in your make-believe world? How do you make it real?

I do a little something called acting.

Mostly, I use three techniques from the Method acting approach as taught by Lee Strasberg. These basic techniques are sense memory, emotional recall, and substitution. I figure if these techniques are good enough for Dustin Hoffman, Al Pacino, and Robert De Niro, then they are good enough for me. You will not find an in-depth discussion of Strasberg's Method here, but I am going tell you my understanding of sense memory, emotional recall, and substitution and how I use these techniques to help me see the world through my character's eyes.

Let's look at each technique separately.

Sense Memory

Sense memory is the recall of sensual experiences from your real life. Sensual experiences like the scent of an ex-lover's perfume, the sound of a song you learned in kindergarten, or pretty much anything you have experienced with any of your five senses during your lifetime.

When using the technique of sense memory, you imagine a sensual experience from your real life in great detail. You recall every sensual aspect of the experience—sight, smell, touch, sound and taste—therefore, recreating the original sensual experience with your imagination. If you practice using sense memory enough, you literally feel the sensations again while using the technique. The major benefit to using the sense memory technique is that this reexperiencing of sensual stimuli increases your belief in the world of the scene. Think about it. If you say you are in a hot barn and start to reexperience the sensation of heat on your skin, then you are going to increase your belief in the world of the scene. You won't just be saying where you are in the scene—you will be experiencing the environment with your senses.

But there's more. When you reexperience a sense memory, it can trigger a powerful and authentic emotional response. Having a powerful and authentic emotional response to a sense memory also increases belief in the world of the scene.

Mastering the sense memory technique is not easy. It takes practice and concentration to truly reexperience stimuli from your real life, but what could be better training for an improviser than to practice remembering how sensual experiences felt? To touch, smell, see, taste, and hear experiences from your past. To recall the stimuli in such detail that it feels like you are experiencing it again, here and now, during the scene. Then to have that sense memory trigger real feelings attached to the memory.

That sounds to me just like what we are trying to do when we improvise—trying to make what we are imagining into something real.

Sense memory uses your life experience to help you create real emotions in the imaginary world of the scene. With practice, you will get better at accessing your sense memory. Eventually, you will be able to spontaneously use this technique to create whatever emotion you want. If you want to create the authentic emotion of joy, all you have to do is pull up the sense memory that creates that real emotional response. Explore your personal sense memories, and you will discover a wealth of authentic emotional responses to use in scene work whenever you want. This is what actors do; they condition themselves to be able to pull up an authentic emotion whenever a scene needs it, and one of the techniques you can use to pull up an emotion is sense memory.

So, that is one major benefit to developing skill with the sense memory technique—you can store sense memories that create a specific emotion. You can create a personal library of emotions caused by sense memory and use them in scenes whenever they are needed. But there is something even better when it comes to developing your skill with sense memory; the real power is when you use it without knowing what your emotional response will be. In every scene I do, every time I visualize the environment, pantomime an object, or imagine a song playing on the radio, I am engaging in sense memory. As I use my imagination to see the environment, touch the object, and hear the song, I am using sense memory, and then I just go with it. All these imagined stimuli are based on sense memories, and as I said before, sense memories cause authentic emotional response. So, when I imagine I am seeing, hearing, or touching something in a scene, I am using sense memory without even knowing what my emotional response is going to be, and because there is no script for the scene, any emotional response triggered by my sense memory will be the right one.

Cultivating your skill with sense memory helps you do two important things. First, it trains you to imagine the sensual experiences of the scene in detail, and second, it teaches you to allow these imagined sensual experiences to trigger your authentic emotional response. In other words, sense memory helps you to believe your make-believe. I utilize this technique every time I improvise (see page 206 for sense memory exercises).

Emotional Recall

Now, let's take a look at emotional recall, or as it is sometimes called, affective memory. When an actor employs emotional recall, he/she uses the sense memory technique to recreate the sensual stimuli that were present during an emotional experience in their real life. So, you have to learn how to use sense memory before you can use emotional recall.

Here is the basic process of using emotional recall. You think of an event or experience in your real life that was emotionally profound, like when your dad hugged you after a big game or when your husband proposed to you. After you pick the event or experience, you use sense memory to recreate all the stimuli that were present. Here is the weird part: you do not focus on the emotions caused by the memory, you focus on the specific sensual experiences you felt during the event. You focus on these sense memories until they become real again and you reexperience them. It will be as if you were back in time, having the experience again. Then the authentic emotions will happen. The emotions are a result of reexperiencing all the sensual stimuli that were present during the memory, not by trying to feel a specific emotion.

Don't believe me?

Okay, try to feel really sad right now. Try. Go ahead and try to feel sad enough to cry right now. Do it. Try to just feel sad. Try to conjure the real emotion of sadness—enough to cry real tears—right now.

Can't do it, can you? Why? Because trying to feel sad does not make you feel sad. What makes you feel the real emotion of sadness is remembering, in great detail, a specific experience you had earlier in life where you were sad.

Strasberg likened actor training to the way Pavlov conditioned dogs. In Pavlov's famous experiment, he conditioned dogs to salivate in response to the sound of a bell, because every time he rang the bell, he gave them food. So, the sound of the bell triggered the sense memory of taste, causing the dogs to have the emotional recall of eating and the real physical response of salivating. Yep, I just compared actor training to the training of dogs, but you see my point—if dogs can do it, you can do it. You can use the emotional recall technique to condition your emotional response to sense memory. If you master this technique, you can create any emotion authentically on command (see page 212 for emotional recall exercises).

Substitution

Let's say you have mastered emotional recall. You can use sense memory to recreate the stimuli that were present during an emotionally profound moment in your life. And when you reexperience these sense memories, they create authentic emotions. Great—what do you do with all these real emotions?

You use them during scene work.

You substitute your real emotions for your character's emotions. You fuse your real feelings to your character. When you do this, the emotions you feel during the scene will be real for you and will seem real to the audience because they are real. You used emotional recall to make sure they were genuine and used substitution to fuse them to your character.

You can train yourself to use substitution anytime the scene demands it. If the scene demands that your character feel sadness, you can drop into your real sadness by using emotional recall and then substitute your real feelings for the character's emotions. And you won't be faking it—you will believe that you are sad, because you actually will be sad. Like I said before, acting is believing (see page 217 for substitution exercises).

So, now you know about three techniques you can use to help you believe in the world of your scene: sense memory, emotional recall, and substitution. They are not easy to learn, but they are worth the effort. They are how I create belief in the scenes I improvise, and believing in your world makes everything easier.

Chapter 6
Stage 2 of the Scenic Structure

Exploring Character Point of View to Discover Your Primary Emotional Drive

So . . . you have fleshed out a scenic agreement with your partner. You have *yes and*-ed each other's ideas until all five of the scenic elements are defined. You know who you are, where you are, and a little bit about why you are there. And by using some acting method, you even believe in your world and are seeing everything through your character's eyes.

What happens next?

You are ready for stage two of the scenic structure. You are ready to explore your character's point of view about their world to discover their Primary Emotional Drive. Your character's Primary Emotional Drive is the feeling that makes them do what they do. In actor speak, it is called your character's objective or motivation, but those terms never worked for me. I like to think that my character has a basic need that is discovered in the scene and that they experience that need through their emotions. This primary emotion drives them to either feel it more if it feels good or feel it less if it feels bad. It is a feeling that makes you do stuff—that is why I call it a Primary Emotional Drive.

All right, so how do you figure out your character's Primary Emotional Drive?

After you get the scenic elements defined, you want to really dive in and explore your character's point of view. That is why we are defining the scenic elements in the first place—to have your character feel something based on this make-believe world. In fact, that is when you know you have built out the scenic elements enough to form an agreement—when your character starts to have a point of view about what is happening in the scene.

In a fully formed scenic agreement, the characters have a point of view about everything in their world. Good characters are highly opinionated; they have points of view about everything around them, especially the other characters in the scene. But point of view is not enough; you have to process your character's point of view into something bigger, something more profound. You have to figure out what is behind the feelings and figure out what your character cares about—what makes them tick. If you fully explore your point of view and figure out why your character feels the way they feel, then you will discover your character's Primary Emotional Drive.

How do you explore?

You do stuff in the scene the way your point of view makes you feel. It's just that easy. Yep, just go ahead and do whatever your character wants to do while you feel your point of view. Go ahead and ask the girl out while feeling fear she will turn you down, or order a glass of wine while feeling superiority toward the waiter. Do and say specific stuff, and allow your point of view to color how you do what you do.

You won't feel the same way about everything in your world. You will have different points of view about different stuff in the scene, just like in your real life. Here's an example: let's say your character is a prisoner on death row who is enjoying a perfectly cooked steak as his last meal. Your character will have a negative point of view about his impending execution and a positive point of view about his perfect steak. Explore both of these contrasting points of view and see what you discover.

Characters also feel the way they feel at various levels of intensity. In the death row example, the negative "I'm gonna die" point of view could be at a much higher intensity than the positive "damn, that's a nice steak" point of view. There are no right or wrong points of view; we just want them based on the world of the scene and explored through the character's behavior. That is how you explore—by doing stuff.

Here is the tricky part about point of view and heightening: not every character point of view gets heightened during a scene. There are plenty of character points of view that are just part of the basic scenic agreement. Point of view is one of the scenic elements, after all. What we want is for our character to discover a specific point of view that becomes more and more intense over time. We call this point of view that grows in intensity during the scene the character's Primary Emotional Drive, and it is the Primary Emotional Drive that gets heightened.

Here is an example of how you could explore character point of view to discover Primary Emotional Drive and then heighten:

> First, you form a scenic agreement with your partner. Let's say you create a scene with two 20-something-year-old women getting ready for a night on the town. They are hanging out at one of the women's apartments, getting dressed, and discussing how excited they are about their impending night out. So, in this example, the point of view of "excited about going out" is part of the initial scenic agreement. The characters can explore this point of view by doing stuff in an excited way. So far, we don't know what feeling is going to be heightened, it could be the mutual excitement that both characters feel at the top of the scene or it could be some other Primary Emotional Drive they discover through their exploration.
>
> At this point in the scene, usually one character does something that is the catalyst that causes an effect in another character. Let's say one of the women in our example discovers, through her exploration, that she is so

excited to be going out tonight because she finally feels free of her last boyfriend. Her general excitement develops into an almost wild abandon as she fantasizes about the adventure this night will bring. And let's say her scene partner is affected by this wild abandon, and she becomes a little worried for her friend. Now, through the exploration of point of view, both characters have discovered their Primary Emotional Drive. One character's Primary Emotional Drive is "freedom-inspired wild abandon," and the other character's is "worry for her friend."

The characters are in a cause-and-effect relationship; the wild abandon in one character causes worry in the other. I would say that both of these characters have found their Primary Emotional Drive, and for the rest of the scene, they would do things because of that feeling. If the feeling is good, like wild abandon, then the character will do stuff to feel that way more. If the feeling is bad, like worry, then the character will do stuff to feel that way less. Just like in real life.

So, to review, you form a scenic agreement with your partner. That scenic agreement includes character point of view. The character points of view are explored through behavior and become more specific. Then one character does something that causes a reaction in the other character(s). This character's reaction declares some kind of emotional point of view. Now both characters have a strong emotional point of view, either discovered through exploration or caused by their scene partner. These emotional points of view or feelings motivate the character's behavior and are heightened throughout the scene. I call these feelings that motivate a character's behavior their Primary Emotional Drive.

The exploration of point of view and discovery of the characters' Primary Emotional Drive is the second stage of the scenic structure. It is the sauce. Once you discover the character's Primary Emotional Drive, you know what you are going to heighten for the rest of the scene.

Character Point of View:
A Little Goes a Long Way

Before we move onto heightening, or stage three of the scenic structure, let's talk about how too much character point of view at the top can kill a scene. When I tell students that their goal in scene work is to explore character point of view to discover their Primary Emotional Drive, they often forget about the other four scenic elements. They forget the whole noodles-and-sauce approach and go straight for the sauce. So, it is important to remind the players that they need to establish all five of the scenic elements at the top of a scene—not just character point of view.

I'm not saying don't walk on stage and rant and rave. This book does not work that way. Go ahead and do it; start with character point of view all you want. Starting with point of view can be a good thing—you have done something specific with your body and voice to figure out what you are make-believing. Just don't act like your job is done because you have an emotional state. Keep working together with your partner on building the agreement until everyone knows what is going on in the world of the scene. Give your emotion some context by establishing all five of the scenic elements every time you improvise so the audience can get involved in your story and care about what happens to your character.

Because (and I might lose a couple of you here) even if you start a scene with an emotional state, you still have to build your agreement. It is called "point of view" for a reason. A point of view is a way a character sees something—another character, an event, environment—anything. "Happy" is not a point of view. You have to have a reason for the feeling for it to be a point of view. "Happy because my wife got home early from work" is a point of view or a way I see something. That is what a point of view is—a way to see a thing.

Starting a scene with an emotional state is a great way to initiate and can lead you to point of view, as long as you establish the reason for your feeling. You have to fill in some of the blanks in order to build a scenic agreement. One of the blanks you need to fill in is why are you are experiencing your emotional state.

Here is an example of a point of view: I am happy because my wife came home early from work. My wife coming home early from work is the reason I am happy. It is my "because." Creating a reason for my emotional state fills in a ton of the blanks that I need to know in order to believe in the world of the scene. When you start creating your emotion's because, you are working to establish your point of view. If I choose to be happy because my wife came home early from work, then a whole bunch of make-believe comes with that.

> I know where I am: home
> I know who my scene partner is: my wife
> I know how I feel about her getting home early: happy

If I know all that, then I have a real shot at success in the scene.

Here is a little equation to help you remember how to create character point of view: Emotion + Because = Point of View.

So go ahead and start scenes with character point of view all you want; just remember, if you do, keep adding scenic elements until everyone understands what is happening.

Why am I going on and on about this like it is a huge problem? Because I have seen thousands of scenes destroyed by too much character point of view at the top.

Why?

Often players get so involved with how their character feels in the scene that they forget to share the information about why they feel that way. In these scenes, character point of view literally overpowers the scenic agreement and stops it from happening. Few, if any, other scenic elements are established in these scenes because one of the characters is completely focused on themselves and how they feel.

It's hard to build a scenic agreement with your partner if you are only focused on yourself.

The Actor Disease

During my 20 years of teaching improv, balancing point of view with the other scenic elements has been the hardest thing for my students to learn. The majority of my students are not actors and often have some natural fear of performance. This fear creates anxiety, and they project that onto the scene. So, it makes some sense that non-actors have to overcome this anxiety before they can stop projecting the negativity it causes onto the scene.

What does not make sense is that the 10 percent of my students who are actors share the same problem of starting negative. They are not afraid of performing, but they still have a negative point of view of their partner before the scene even starts. I have seen this type of behavior so much in trained actors that I have a term for it. I call it the Actor Disease.

Why that name?

Whenever I have someone in class with traditional acting training, they almost always force negative character point of view at the top scenes. It does not matter what they are given by their partner. They always find a way to have intensely negative feelings about that person or activity and then—bang—we have an argument on our hands. What's worse is they are usually blind to their penchant for negativity and just think they are bad improvisers because their scenes often fail. The scenes fail because an argument between characters that has no context is unearned and won't make us care. We won't know why the characters are arguing, so we won't care. Without the noodles, we won't care about the sauce.

Here is a little test to see if you have the Actor Disease. I am going to give you three initial offers for a scene, and you make up what the second line would be.

> 1. (While driving a car) "Hey, let me just say, I am looking forward to meeting your parents."
>
> 2. (While clearing the table) "Mary's new boyfriend seemed nice; tonight was fun."
>
> 3. (While shining a flashlight) "This old house is so cool on the inside."

If all of your responses to these three initial offers were negative, then you might be infected with the Actor Disease.

Why?

Because in my little test, there is nothing negative in the make-believe world that is being offered to you. All three initial offers above establish some reality and a touch of positive point of view. The world of the scene still needs to be built out, but if you regularly respond to neutral or positive offers with a negative point of view, then how you feel might not be based on what you are getting from your partner. And if you don't want to base your choices on what your partner is giving you, then perhaps you should work alone.

Why do these trained actors have an uncontrollable habit of starting negative?

Actors have been taught that all theatre is conflict, and when they improvise, they race to it. Trained actors want to feel something strong and fast; otherwise, they are lost. They rely on a script to give them what they do and say, and they focus completely on how they feel while doing what the script demands. However, improv demands that the actors cooperate to define the world of the scene. Actors from scripted theatre often skip this step and go directly to how they feel about the world before it is even defined. And honestly, I think actors like to play negative emotions. It feels dramatic. It feels like they are really doing something. To me, it just seems like they are controlled by their need to be seen as talented. I would be much more impressed if they just focused on their partner and cooperated to build a sound scenic agreement.

I have figured out the two main reasons why inexperienced improvisers start negative. They are either freaking out and anxious because make-believe is alien to them, or they have the Actor Disease and start with how they feel without helping to build the agreement.

You might think an easy fix to the problem would be to tell these improvisers, "Don't start negative," but you can't learn what to do by being taught what not to do. Furthermore, there is nothing wrong with starting negative. We just want your negativity to be created by something inside the world of the scene, not your anxiety or your Actor Disease. We want what you do in a scene to be a choice, and that is the real problem here—these improvisers are predetermining something that should be spontaneous. How our character feels should be discovered inside the make-believe world of the scene and not influenced by the real world.

So, what is the cure for the Actor Disease?

I have found that the diagnosis is often the cure. Actors are used to making adjustments in their performance based on direction. If you tell an actor that they start almost every scene with a negative character point of view, even when they get a positive offer from their partner, they can make an adjustment. If you tell the actor they are putting too much focus on the self and not enough on what they are getting from their partner, they can make an adjustment. The actor won't change their behavior overnight, but their awareness of starting negative will grow. And once actors recognize their negativity at the tops of scenes not as a choice, but predetermined by their need to feel conflict with their partner, then they usually get better.

Chapter 7
Stage 3 of the Scenic Structure

Heightening

Yay! We made it to stage three of the scenic structure: Heightening. We finally got to the fun part: The part of the scene where you know what you are make-believing, you have explored your character's point of view, discovered your Primary Emotional Drive, and now it is time to heighten.

But before we get into the details of how you do it, let's define heightening.

Heightening is taking whatever is happening in a scene and making it more. If a character likes what is happening, I try to make it even better; if they don't like what is happening, I try to make it worse. And, hopefully, that is what my partner is doing for me as well—figuring out how I feel about what is going on and making me feel that way more. So, we could say that heightening is doing something to make the scene more of what it already is.

So how do you do it? What exactly are you doing when you heighten?

I believe there are basically two ways to heighten what is going on in the scene. One way is to repeat and intensify the cause and effect between the characters, and the other way is to raise the stakes of the dramatic situation. Those are the two techniques I use to heighten a scene.

Let's deal with repeating and intensifying cause and effect first.

I know that "repeating and intensifying cause and effect" might sound a little scientific method-y for some people, but all I mean by it is for you to keep doing whatever you are doing that is getting a response from your partner.

Usually, cause and effect starts to happen during stage two of the scene, when the characters are exploring their point of view by doing stuff. While you are exploring your point of view, something will happen to your character that causes them to respond. That's what cause and effect is in terms of improv scene work—something happens (that's the cause), and you respond (that's the effect). In order to heighten, we need a character to cause an effect in another character, and then we need that cause repeated with intensified effect.

There is something else you should know about this whole "repeat and intensify cause and effect" process. Eventually, that thing that causes you to respond in the scene needs to be your partner. Sooner or later, you need to get into a cause and effect relationship with your partner; that way, when your partner does stuff in the scene, your point of view will be altered. Now it does not matter what specific thing your partner did that caused you to be effected, we just want more of the cause and more of the effect. More cause that results in effecting you in an ever-increasing way.

Once we see a specific cause that results in the effect of your point of view being altered, we want to see other things in the scene that make you feel your point of view—more. We want to see that over and over again. We also want the cause-and-effect process to work on all the characters in a scene—not just one character being altered by one other character. Everyone is invited to the cause-and-effect party; that way, every character in a scene can be altered by every other character.

The repetition of cause resulting in increased effect is your bread and butter when it comes to heightening. Most of the time, it's what you do to heighten scenes.

But you don't just repeat the same cause over and over again; we want to see many causes that heighten the way the characters feel. We want to see more specific stuff one character does that affects the other character(s) in an increasingly intense way. It does not matter what the characters do, as long as the result of their behavior is another character feeling the way they feel—more.

Repeating and intensifying the cause of the effect will naturally intensify a character's point of view. It is this intensification of a character's point of view that leads to the discovery of their Primary Emotional Drive. Once a character encounters their Primary Emotional Drive, the improviser knows their job for the rest of the scene: Heighten that drive.

Here's an example of this process at work:

> Let's say you start a scene with your character sitting in their apartment, studying for a test, and your scene partner is sitting close by, reading a book. So, at the top of the scene, both of you are just sitting and reading. Then, after a few seconds your scene partner starts to laugh at something she read in the book. Her laughter is interrupting your studies, and this is making you a little mad.

Now we have some cause and effect. Her laughter is causing the effect of you getting a little mad. Once we see a specific cause and effect that results in you forming a point of view; then we want to see more causes that result in the same effect. We want to see other things that make you feel your point of view—more. More specific stuff that your roommate does that makes you angrier. Really, it could be anything; your roomie could do just about anything, as long as the result of her doing it made you madder.

Let's return to the scene:

> Your studies have just been interrupted by your housemate's laughter. You are getting mad, but your housemate's laughter stops before you say anything, so you go back to your studies. A few moments pass and your housemate laughs again, this time even louder, and you get a little

more upset. This time you glare at your partner, and she says, "I'm sorry," and closes the book. You return to your studies, and for a moment your partner sits in silence. Then your scene partner grabs her laptop, opens it up, and starts to check her email. As she reads the first email, she starts to laugh. Her laughter interrupts your studies again, and you are now very upset.

In this example, your partner initially repeated the cause of laughing at her book to get an increased response from you, and then she found another specific cause, her email, to get a heightened effect. It works well to repeat the original cause once or twice so everyone can get on the same page, but then we want to see different specific stuff that becomes the cause. It works best if the new specific cause makes sense based on what the original cause was, like in our example: your scene partner laughing while she reads her email is kind of similar to her laughing while she reads her book. But in any case, we want your scene partner to keep doing specific stuff to interrupt your studies.

Honestly, the world will sit and watch your studies being interrupted by your laughing roomie for hours. All you need to do in order to keep the scene fun to play and fun to watch is drop into your Primary Emotional Drive of frustration because your studies are being interrupted. Drop in and commit to your frustration, and you will see the world through your character's eyes and speak with your character's authentic voice. Your character's natural desire to get what they want—uninterrupted time to study—will heighten the scene. You will do stuff in the scene because of your motivating Primary Emotional Drive, and your scene partner will do stuff because of theirs. Your scene partner will become the cause to your effect, and you will live the scene moment by moment.

You won't be thinking, "What am I going to say next?" You will be thinking character thoughts. You will be feeling the character's feelings, doing and saying what you need to do and say in order to get what you want.

I call this type of heightening—where you use the process of repeating and intensifying cause and effect between the characters—the heightening of point of view. I don't tell students the name of this type of heightening until after I describe the step-by-step method.

Why?

Because I want them to focus on the process of repeating and intensifying the cause and effect rather than the outcome, which is a heightened character point of view. Heightened character point of view is the end result of a lot of cause and effect, and you can't skip the steps and jump to the end. So, even though the thing we see being heightened is the character point of view, in order to achieve that goal, you have to think of it as a process of repetition and intensification of cause and effect.

Heightening Point of View Using Relationship Componentry

So, establishing cause and effect between the characters is the key to heightening point of view. Let me share with you my favorite way to create cause and effect. I think you get to cause and effect in scenes by exploring the relationship between the characters.

You have heard that a million times, right? I mean, haven't we all been in an improv class and heard the teacher say to us while we are trying to do a scene:

> "Focus on the relationship. Figure out who these people are to each other."

I know I have, and don't get me wrong, I think that is very good advice, but just focusing on the relationship and trying to figure out who these people are to each other never really worked for me. The relationship was just way too big of a concept for me to wrap my mind around. Relationship is a word that gets thrown around so much when students are learning about improv that it starts to lose its meaning.

Trying to figure out my relationship with my scene partner was hard. I wanted to explore the relationship between the characters, but I didn't know how. Sure, I could label the characters in the scene as doctor/patient or husband/wife, but that did not get me to that super-connected, cause-and-effect relationship with my partner that I wanted so much.

So, as you might be able to guess by now, when I encounter something that I think is super-hard to do in improv, I create a little system to help me do it. That's exactly what I did to help myself explore relationship in scene work. I created a little system that I call relationship "componentry."

Before we get into my little system that helps me explore relationship, let's revisit my definition for relationship from chapter 3. I am throwing that word around a lot and don't want it to lose its meaning. When I say relationship in the context of improv scene work, I mean the following step-by-step process:

> Relationship is the process of defining a set of **Relationship Components,** or ways characters are connected. These connections create a cause and effect between the characters inside the context of the world of the scene. This cause and effect between characters is repeated and heightened and yields **the Dynamic.**

So, when I am "focusing on relationship" and "figuring out who these people are to each other," I follow this step-by-step process:

> Step 1
> Define the ways the characters are connected. I call these relationship components.
>
> Step 2
> These connections create cause and effect between the characters.
>
> Step 3
> Repeat and intensify the cause and effect.
>
> Step 4
> Repeat steps 1–3 to yield the Dynamic.

Let's take a closer look at the steps. First, we define ways we are connected to each other. Establishing these Relationship

Components, like our history with our scene partner, is the first step. As these connections are established, they have an effect, in the moment, on the characters. You know, you do or say something specific and the other guy reacts. When the other guy reacts, he does or says something specific and then you react. The stuff the characters are doing to each other creates a cause and effect. Then, that cause and effect is repeated and heightened. The repetition and intensification of the cause and effect acts as a catalyst and creates the Dynamic. When I say "relationship" in terms of improv scene work, I mean this entire process—a process that yields the Dynamic.

What is the Dynamic?

The Dynamic is hard to define. It is not something you control—it is something you discover. It is something you play with. But a more textbook definition would be that it's the specific way these characters interact in this moment, the effect they have on each other, and how they change.

That sounds like fun, right? Let's take a look at how to do relationship-based scene work by discovering and playing with the Dynamic.

Before we get going, remember that the Dynamic is the result of a bunch of hard work. You can't just jump up there and say, "Give me some Dynamic, I wanna play." You have to do the hard work first. You have to pay for the fun, so let's get to it.

The first step in creating the Dynamic is using a little system called Relationship Components to establish connections between characters. This system will help you figure out how characters are connected to each other in their make-believe world. As you establish these connections, you will encounter cause and effect, and as you play with cause and effect, you will discover the Dynamic.

Here is my little system:

Relationship Components (or ways characters are connected):

HISTORY
EMOTION
STATUS
PHYSICALITY
SENSUALITY
SPACE

Each of these components is a way characters can be connected. When one of these connections is made, both characters are affected. It's the combination of these connections that affect the way characters behave toward one another. The way characters behave toward one another and how characters are altered by that behavior results in cause and effect. You repeat and intensify cause and effect to discover the Dynamic.

As you can see, the steps you follow to explore relationship in scene work are the same ones you follow to heighten point of view in a scene. So, as far as I am concerned, heightening point of view and exploring relationship are the same thing.

Let's take a look at each component, one at a time.

By the way, when I teach Relationship Componentry, I always work in the order below:

History: The characters' shared past with each other.

When you have a history with someone, you treat them in a way that is informed by your shared past. This is true in the real world, as well as in improv. So, here is a way to use history to help create connections and cause and effect: imagine your past to play your present.

Try it.

First, try remembering a person from your real life who makes you feel something specific. Make sure it is someone who evokes strong feelings for you. Visualize their face, recreate their voice, and imagine what they might say to you. Work to really see, hear, and feel that person as if they were in the same room with you right now. Imagine that person right in front of you.

How would you behave around them?

This is the way a real-life history alters the way you relate to another person; however, you aren't limited by your real life once you learn how to "play" a history toward your partner—you can play any history you imagine.

Try it.

Imagine a specific make-believe past with someone, anything with some real flavor, like an ex-lover who you are not over yet or old boss who gave you your first real shot. These kinds of histories with your scene partner make you care about what they do and say.

If you make-believe that your scene partner is the ex-lover you are not over yet or the old boss that gave you your first real shot, then you will know how you feel about them. You will also care deeply about what they do and say. And because you care deeply, then they will alter you. Being altered by your partner will lead you to cause and effect, and cause and effect will help you discover the Dynamic.

Perhaps you have heard this from an improv teacher before: "It helps if the characters know each other." It's good advice, but I put it this way:

Imagine your past with your scene partner to play your present.

Emotion: The moment-by-moment change in a character's feelings about the other characters.

If history is the brain of relationship, emotion is the blood. Emotionally responding to our scene partner, moment-by-moment, is proof the characters are connected.

It is our emotional response to our scene partner's behavior that gives that behavior meaning. My scene partner could do just about anything—they could pour a cup of coffee, kiss me, or start the car—whatever, but it doesn't mean anything until it causes a reaction in me. My emotional reaction can change what the behavior means for the characters. If my scene partner kisses me and I slap her face in anger, we are connected in a much different way than if I kiss back.

Whenever we see the behavior of one character change the emotional state of another, we see the connection. One character does something, and the other character emotionally reacts—now we can see the cause and effect.

Here is a way to use the component of emotion to heighten your scene partner: chase what changes.

If you do something, and it changes your partner's emotional state, then chase it. Chase that feeling in your partner by doing similar stuff to get a heightened response. Repeat and intensify the cause to get a heightened effect.

Status: The rank of each character's importance, in relation to every other character, in the world of the scene.

In my experience, status is the most misunderstood Relationship Component. People think status is something a character has, like if they are a king, they have high status, or if they are a drug dealer, then they have low status. But this is not true. Status is not something a character has—it is something a character does.

Character status is active and has much more to do with character movement, eye contact, and posture than it does with a label like "king" or "drug dealer." You could easily be a low-status king if you were afraid to look your servants in the eyes, and a drug dealer can play high status to a judge if he speaks slowly, keeps his head perfectly still, and holds eye contact.

Another tricky thing about status is that it is relative. In every scene, the characters are connected in a status hierarchy or pecking order. A hierarchy that helps define who the characters are to one another. For example, you might be playing a high-status character with slow, deliberate movement and lingering eye contact, but if your scene partner plays higher status, then you will be seen as lower status. You will be low status relative to your scene partner, even though you are trying to play high status. Your character's relative lower status to your scene partner tells us a lot about who you are to each other.

In my opinion, there are two ways to look at status in a scene: the circumstance and the characters.

Let's say the circumstance of the scene is you meeting with the doctor who is going to operate on your brain. Now, you would think the doctor would typically play high status to you in that situation. If this situation happened in real life, the doctor would be most important. Your life depends on that doctor, so that is going to affect the way you relate to him. But if that same brain surgeon is standing, say, third in line at Starbucks, and he really wants a latte, then he might play low status to the barista. In both of these examples, character status is generated by the dramatic situation or circumstance. Whoever has the power in the situation and is willing to use it is seen as high status.

But there is no appropriate status for a character in any given situation. What if I was in that same brain surgeon scene and the doctor was fidgety and afraid to make eye contact with me? What if I had to comfort him and tell him that as long as he tried his best, it doesn't matter if I live or die? Well, then that surgeon would be low status to my relative high status, even though the dramatic situation would lead us to believe the opposite.

Status is also in constant flux; the little things people do to maintain, increase, or diminish their status constantly rearrange the pecking order of the characters in the scene. Just because a character starts a scene with high status doesn't mean they will stay high status during the whole scene.

Status, more than any other component, is something you need to try on for size. Remember, status is something you do, so try some of the status exercises on page 179 and see how much fun you can have playing with status.

I call these first three Relationship Components—**History**, **Emotion**, and **Status**—the *big three* because I use them the most.

I group the next three Relationship Components—**Physicality, Sensuality, and Space**—together because they deal with the actors' physical form and things their bodies experience sensually. So, think of Physicality, Sensuality, and Space as one big messy component dealing with your body in space and what it is sensing.

Physicality: How the player's body—its shape, gestures, and contact with other actors—relates to the other players in the scene. How the player's movement in space and its tempo and direction relates to the other players in the scene.

> The actor's bodies, how they move, and how they touch each other are the basic building blocks of relationship. If two people are hugging, both with their eyes closed and smiling, we know they are emotionally close. No one has to tell us this, and they don't have to speak to communicate it. The physicality of their two bodies tells us how they are connected.
>
> Contact is not always necessary, either. Hold both hands straight up in the air and widen your eyes while facing your partner and—presto—they are robbing you. You are connected to that person, and the situation is ripe for cause and effect. You may even establish it before you ever open your mouth.
>
> The desire to physically relate to my partner before I even speak was the origin of the Join technique to start scenes discussed in chapter 4. That is what the Join is—playing with physicality at the top of scenes to discover how you are connected to your partner. But you don't have to stop using this component once the scene starts. Every moment of a scene is filled with physicality that tells us something about the characters' relationship, so allow yourself to play with physicality throughout the scene.

Sensuality: Any sensual stimulation experienced by a character caused by another character.

> We are connected to the people who stimulate our senses. Touch, taste, smell, see, or hear your scene partner—

any of these experiences will tell you who you are to one another. What's more is that this sensual experience will change your state of being. This sensual experience caused by your partner will alter you.

Imagine your scene partner's skin is hot to the touch, and you may begin to nurse them back to health. Smell another woman's perfume on your scene partner, and he instantly becomes a cheating husband; I promise, your state of being will change.

Our senses connect us to our world as we relate to what we experience. Make-believe that your scene partner is stimulating any of your senses, and you will be altered. To do this, you will need to cultivate your sense memory. Sense memory is the kinesthetic knowledge of how sensory experiences make your body feel—something like the body's memory of how it feels to get punched in the stomach or how it feels to jump into a pool of cold water. Actors work hard to develop their sense memory, which helps them recreate the reality of a sensory experience in scene work. Sense memory is a basic skill you must have in order to make-believe, as well as to play with the component of sensuality. Sense memory is discussed in chapters 5 and 11.

Space: The spatial relationship among the players, the distance between players, where each player is focused, and the levels of space players put themselves.

We are not only connected by contact; we are also connected by the space between our body and the bodies around us. Choosing to stay far away from your scene partner says just as much about who you are to each other as constant contact.

Let's say your partner places a chair center stage and sits in it. Where you put yourself in space in relation to this player could tell you and your partner everything you need to know about your world. Place another chair alongside the first chair, and you will be in a very different scene than if you pace urgently upstage of the chair.

The bodies in space create pictures that can tell us who we are in the world of the scene. We want to use our spatial relationship with our partner to create meaning. If one player is pacing back and forth upstage of a seated player, we want that spatial relationship to define who these characters are to each other.

If the spatial relationship changes, we want that to have meaning as well. The spatial relationship among players is constantly changing from moment to moment. As players, we are constantly moving around the space and changing the spatial relationship. We just want the change of the spatial relationship among the players to have meaning for the relationship. We want each new arrangement of the player's bodies in space to mean something.

Honestly, bodies in space always have meaning. Improvisers are just untrained in how to play with the component of space to discover stuff about their relationship to their scene partner. Learn more about playing with space on page 158.

Okay, those are the six Relationship Components, or ways characters are connected. I think it is important to be able to recognize these connections and be able to establish them at will. When I improvise, I am constantly doing specific stuff to establish a Relationship Component with my scene partner. Honestly, at the top of a scene, I have this little mantra going in my head:

> "Use components to make connections, be altered by your scene partner, repeat, intensify, and encounter the Dynamic."

After 25 years of doing improv, I am still learning how to do that simple process.

Relationship Components and Environment

So, you just learned about my little system to create connections among the characters, but we also have a relationship to our environment.

That's right. Explore any of these components and you will learn more about how you relate to your scene partner. But you don't just relate to your scene partner—you relate to your environment, too. Characters are certainly connected to their environment by Relationship Componentry. Just as you can play a component to establish a connection to your scene partner, you can do the same to your environment.

We have history with the places of our lives, and so do the characters we create. Imagine returning to a park where you were mugged. That history will shape how you feel in that environment. You may be very scared every time you return to that park.

Environment and objects also have status. Your boss's office and his desk retain his status, even when he is not there. So, yes, you can play low status to a desk.

The obvious connection we have to environment is sensuality. If you are outside at night during the winter, then you are going to be sensually altered. You are going to shiver, rub your hands together, and watch the foggy breath coming out of your mouth because it's cold. Any environment could stimulate your senses if you made the choice.

Our relationship with our environment differs from our relationship with our scene partner in that it is not a two-way street. Your environment will have a cause-and-effect relationship with you, but you will most likely not have a cause-and-effect relationship with your environment. However, even though the cause-and-effect relationship is one-sided, the effect the environment has on the characters can still be repeated and heightened to discover the Dynamic of the scene.

Relationship Components are just ways you can be connected to your partner and to your environment. See page 171 for exercises that help you play Relationship Components to your environment.

The Other Way to Heighten: Raising the Stakes

Most of the time, a scene is heightened by repeating and intensifying cause and effect between the characters. In these scenes, we are using the technique of heightening point of view. As a character's point of view becomes more intense, they discover their Primary Emotional Drive. That is what we are watching in these heightened-point-of-view scenes—a character's ever-increasing drive to get what they want. This type of heightening focuses on character, but there is another way to heighten.

You can heighten a scene by raising the stakes of what is happening in the dramatic situation. This type of heightening focuses on the circumstance of the scene rather than character point of view. To raise the stakes, you need to increase the significance and risk of the events taking place during the scene. If, in a scene, you are having a mundane argument with your boyfriend about what movie to go see, you can raise the stakes of the dramatic situation by saying you want to break up. You just changed the circumstance of the dramatic situation. This is no longer an argument about what movie to go see, this is a break-up scene, and it just got heightened by becoming more significant and risky for the characters.

Here's another example of how to raise the stakes of the dramatic situation:

> Let's say the scene starts with a man and a woman waiting in line at a bank. They are holding hands and waiting in silence. We know they are in a bank because at the top of the scene one of the players said something like, "I wonder how much it costs to cash a check at this bank if you don't have an account here." You know, just to make it clear to everyone what they are make-believing. Then, after a few moments, the guy says:
>
> "Sue, I didn't appreciate you making fun of me last night at that dinner party. When we are around other people, you make fun of me, and it hurts my feelings."

> Sue responds:
>
> "Frank, you are oversensitive and need to toughen up."
>
> This also hurts Frank's feelings.

All right, we have some cause and effect going on between the characters, and we could repeat and intensify that to heighten the scene or we could raise the stakes of the dramatic situation.

Let's try to heighten this scene by raising the stakes:

> Now Sue and Frank, while waiting in line at the bank, are having a spat because Frank feels that Sue makes fun of him when they are around other people. Just then, a third character enters the scene and says:
>
> "Hey, Sue, Frank, this bank isn't going to rob itself. I have been waiting in the getaway car for 15 minutes. What is taking so long?"

Now we have a lovers' spat during a bank robbery, and the stakes have been raised. The scene has transformed from what we thought was a couple arguing in a bank into a much more important event in the character's lives. The consequence of the characters' actions in this scene just skyrocketed.

The bank robbery is a new context for the argument. This new, heightened context raises the stakes and changes everything—for the characters and the audience.

Let's look at what this new context changes for the characters.

> Frank and Sue are willing to interrupt their bank robbery to have this argument. Honestly, in this example, the two improvisers who started the scene didn't know they were in the middle of committing a bank robbery until the third character came in and told them. But they know now, and this new context for their argument reveals a lot. Frank and Sue are characters who are willing to jeopardize the robbery because of a lovers' quarrel. They are taking risks in a situation that has great significance to their lives, and

these kinds of characters are fun to play.

Let's look at what this new context changes for the audience.

Setting the argument in the middle of a bank robbery increases risk for the characters and adds tension to the dramatic situation. This event will affect the characters' entire lives; it is much more important than some mundane argument. This makes the audience really want to know what happens next; kind of like when an audience watches a movie, play, or television show and the characters take risks, the tension rises and they watch to find out what happens. Why? Because they care about the characters and the story. Raising the stakes keeps the audience invested in what is happening in the scene.

And I've got some good news about heightening—you can use both techniques at the same time. Yep, you can raise the stakes and heighten point of view in the same scene. Let's rejoin the scene after the stakes have been raised:

> Now Sue, Frank, and the getaway driver are waiting in line. Sue responds to the driver's question of "What is taking so long?" She says:
>
>> "Sorry, we are taking forever. Frank here is getting all weepy because he thinks (in a mocking voice) I make fun of him in front of other people."
>
> This makes Frank a little upset and he says:
>
>> "Really, Sue? You are going to do this now? I can tell you one thing, we are not taking any hostages because you will just make fun of me in front of them."

Now both the character point of view and the dramatic situation have been heightened in the scene. This is literally double the heightening and double the fun.

There is one thing you want to be aware of when you heighten by raising the stakes—you want to make sure you are still making the scene more of what it already is. In the scenic example above, the players established they were in a bank before the third player came on and added the new information that they were robbing the bank. I would say the third player *yes and*-ed the environment of bank. The third player said, "Yes, you are having an argument in a bank, and you are robbing it."

But you can see the kind of jokey damage a player could do with raising the stakes by adding information that creates nothing more than a comic juxtaposition. Think about it. You could walk up to any two characters that are having an argument and say, "Hey, guys, this bank isn't going to rob itself." Just make sure you are walking on to heighten the scene that is already happening; otherwise, you are just trying to be funny.

One last thing about raising the stakes. In the example above, I had a third character come on and add information to create a new context for the scene. This is only one (and, perhaps, a common) way to add the new information. Of course, the characters that are already in the scene can raise the stakes by adding information as well. Any character at any time can choose to raise the stakes by increasing the risk and significance of the dramatic situation.

Why Do We Heighten?

Now we know how to heighten scenes, but why do we do it? What is the benefit? What is the payoff of all this heightening?

I think the payoff is that when a scene is heightened, we get to be surprised by what happens.

That's what we ultimately want, right? To be completely surprised by what happens in the scene. To be shocked by our own behavior, to not be able to believe that you just did or said what you just did or said. And let me tell you, if you heighten the scene enough, sooner or later, you are going to surprise yourself. If you heighten the scene enough, something in the scene is ultimately going to go boom. You or your partner will do or say something that you could never have planned, something completely spontaneous. And wouldn't it be wonderful if something spontaneous and totally unexpected happened during the scenes we create?

Heightening is the catalyst that creates the spontaneous, totally unexpected surprise that we want to happen in our improv scenes.

Here is a way to look at heightening that may help you see my point:

> A scene is like a science experiment. We're throwing all these different chemicals into a test tube. When these chemicals get added, they mix and start to react. Because we have never done this exact experiment before, we have no idea how these chemicals are going to react with each other. Sometimes when the chemicals mix in the test tube, they smoke and fizz. And sometimes they just sit there. And then, to accelerate the chemicals mixing and reacting, we light a Bunsen burner and add some heat to the test tube.
>
> This heat is a catalyst and changes everything. As the temperature rises, the mixture changes. It starts to boil and change color and liquid becomes gas. And remember, we have never combined these exact chemicals in this exact way, and we don't know what is going to happen now that we are adding heat to the mixture.
>
> At this point in the experiment, we have a very unstable, hot mixture that we have never created before. Then the mixture goes boom.

In my scenic theory, heightening is like the heat in that experiment. The heat or the heightening makes the characters do and say things that are completely spontaneous. When you heighten character point of view or raise the stakes of the dramatic situation, it is like you are boiling the chemicals in that test tube, and you will be surprised by what happens in the scene. When a scene gets heightened enough, it changes. The increased tension in the scene causes characters to change their emotional state, causing them to reveal things they would usually never disclose and stop hiding what they really want to say.

When point of view and the stakes get heightened enough, characters will do and say awesome, totally unexpected, and surprising things.

That is why we heighten—to be surprised.

The Problem with Heightening

Now that you know the two classic heightening techniques—heighten point of view and raise the stakes—scenes should take care of themselves, right? Heightening should be easy now.

Nope. Improv is not easy. It takes hard work and practice and what's worse is that lots of times we sabotage our own success by reversing the heightening process.

I have found that right about the time in a scene when the players need to start either raising the stakes or heightening a point of view, this weird thing happens. All the hard work has been done, and the players know what they are make-believing, how they feel, and why they feel that way. The players have explored point of view, resulting in cause and effect, and have discovered their Primary Emotional Drive, and then—poof—they bail on what they have built. They figure out a way to stop feeling the way they feel.

If they are happy with what is going on, they discover something they don't like. If they are angry about something in the scene, their partner will try to make them feel better. If there is some kind of problem the characters are facing, a player will figure out a way to solve it. The players sabotage the scene by finding a way to stop feeing the way they feel or by reducing the stakes. This is the opposite of heightening. This is lowering.

Here's the deal. If you buy into the whole three-stage, scenic-structure thing by building a scenic agreement, then exploring a point of view to discover Primary Emotional Drive, and finally, heighten that drive, when you bail on your point of view, you just have to go find another one. If your character stops feeling the way they feel about what is happening in the scene, then you can't heighten point of view. There is no point of view to heighten.

And improvisers bail on their point of view all the time.

Why do improv actors do this? Why do they figure all this stuff out just to stall the scene by bailing on their point of view?

Two reasons. One is easy to fix. Unfortunately, the other is very hard to overcome . . . but let's try.

Here's the first reason (the one that is easy to fix): they don't know any better. This improviser has yet to figure out that a character's point of view needs to be heightened by cause and effect during the scene. This player is focused on the self and just needs to place more focus on the other—their scene partner. Once this improviser feels some success in scene work by discovering their point of view and relentlessly heightening it, they will be addicted. This is an easy fix.

And here's the other reason (the one that's hard to fix): this other improviser is bailing on their character's point of view because they're judging themselves and the scene. They are watching the scene from the outside and worrying if it's funny or not rather than seeing the world through their character's eyes. It's easy for this improviser to bail on their point of view because they never really believe in the world of the scene. They never really feel the way their character feels because they aren't the character—they are an improviser, on stage, worried about how others view their work. This improviser will bail at the first sign of trouble, and that is a serious problem when it comes to heightening because if you bail on your character's point of view, it is very hard to heighten it.

I don't know why this hard-to-fix problem exists for so many improvisers. Perhaps these improvisers don't have any acting training and see improv as just comedy. Maybe they are afraid of being made fun of if they really transform into the character, but for whatever reason, these improvisers have a block when it comes to being inside the world of the scene. They are focused on the wrong thing—other people's judgment of their work.

I will tell you this right now, and please take it to heart. Judgment will never make you a better improviser. Judgment is just fear—fear of failure, fear of your peers thinking you are foolish for ever thinking you could do improv, fear of what other people think of you, fear of looking like a fool; I could go on, but you get my point.

I know I told you before that there are no don'ts in this book, but I lied; there is one don't in this book. Here it is: don't let fear of other people's judgment or your own self-judgment control what you do in improv. I mean this. Whatever you need to do in order to be free of judgment in the scenes you create—do it.

That is my one *don't*.

Don't judge the improv you create while you are doing it. While you are improvising, don't judge yourself, your scene partner, or the scene. After the show, class, or workshop is over, judge all you want, but not while you are doing it. Because judging yourself, your scene partner, or the scene while you are improvising will never make you a better improviser.

What will make you a better improviser is taking the risk to drop into your character's Primary Emotional Drive and trying to get whatever it is your character wants. Committing to your character's point of view, even if it makes you look stupid, could definitely make you a better improviser. Go ahead and take a risk—drop in, commit, and heighten like a crazy person—what's the worst that could happen? Really, what is your worst-case scenario if you go all out and commit like a crazy person?

Your make-believe scene might not go as well as you wished it had. If that is the worst that can happen, I think it's worth the risk.

Chapter 8
Judgment, Fear, and Courage

Before I get all judgmental about judgment, let me just say that not all judgment is bad. Heck, when we feel good about our work and swell with confidence because we know the scene we just did was awesome, that is judgment, too. When I say, "Judgment will never make you a better improviser," I am not talking about this positive, swell-with-confidence kind of judgment. I am talking about the kind of judgment that freezes you with fear and makes it almost impossible to take the risks you need to take to do your best work.

If you are going to talk about judgment in improv, then you have to talk about fear because that is the downside of judgment. It makes us afraid. We are judgmental of our work because we fear failure. We are judgmental of our work because we are afraid of making fools out of ourselves. In improv, fear and judgment kind of go hand in hand.

So, what I am talking about is the negative kind of judgment that creates fear. And I have found that pretty much everyone who starts to take improv seriously eventually has to deal with their fear of doing it.

Why?

Because when everyone starts out doing improv, they are, on some level, afraid.

The problem with fear is that it can keep you from doing what you want to do. Fear can stop you from taking the risks you need to take to create good improv. It's hard to be playful and spontaneous when you are afraid of looking like a fool. As the improv guru Keith Johnstone put it, "Fear kills fun." In fact, almost every improv teacher I have ever met has something negative to say about fear. So, fear is bad, it is the killer of fun, it makes you the bad kind of judgmental, and we should avoid it at all costs.

Here's the problem with the whole "fear is bad" philosophy: it's completely natural that people who are learning how to improvise are afraid, because improv is hard to do. Improv, by its very nature, takes you out of your comfort zone. Improv is spontaneous. There is no plan and no one is in control and that sounds like something most people would be a little anxious about.

Improv is risky, and being afraid of risky stuff is normal. And what's worse is that qualifying fear as bad does very little to actually reduce the amount of fear a person feels.

I have a contrasting point of view about fear and improv. Fear is just a feeling, and if you actually are afraid, then you can't just deny, reject, or toxify that feeling. No amount of kicking and screaming is going to get you to stop feeling the way you feel, so stop trying and just do stuff even though you are afraid.

Let me use myself as an example. When I started doing improv over 25 years ago, I was crippled by fear and anxiety. I had all these good ideas, and it brought me such joy to improvise, but I was frozen by fear and panic, especially right before a performance. I would constantly think, "Will they like me? Will the scene be funny? Will I look stupid doing this silly make-believe stuff?" To complicate matters, I read all this stuff in improv books about fear literally killing anything fun, and I became very judgmental (the bad kind) of my fear.

I was afraid, and I felt guilty and weak because I was afraid. The fear was in control. The fear had all the power.

Before or during shows, I would feel fear, and then I would become more afraid from worrying that my fear would kill the fun during the show. My fear was literally creating more fear. Before shows, I would be anxious that I would be afraid during the show. I was literally afraid that I was going to be afraid. And then—bang—I would be afraid during the show. Then I would beat myself up afterwards for being afraid.

I was tired of giving my fear all this power.

I was judging myself for being afraid of something basically everyone in the world was afraid of—looking stupid in front of other people. That is a completely natural fear, and I was tired of feeling bad about it. And, for the record, labeling my fear as a "fun killer" had no effect in reducing how afraid I was.

So, I experimented with going into my fear. That's right. When I felt fear, or worse yet, panic, starting to grow inside of me, rather than pushing back against it or feeling bad because everyone in the past told me that you cannot simultaneously do improv and be afraid at the same time, instead of those learned responses to fear, I did this crazy thing. I allowed myself to be afraid, and then I went out there and did what I was going to do anyway—while I was afraid. I did the thing I was afraid of while I was afraid.

I went out there and did some improv even though I was afraid of doing improv.

I was still afraid of all the stuff I was afraid of before; however, I just took action in the face of the fear. That's what courage is—doing something even though you are afraid to do it, taking action in the face of fear.

When I started doing this, two things happened. First, I took the power away from the fear. Fear could not stop me anymore. It was not that I stopped being afraid, it was just that I could act while I was afraid. Secondly, because now I was no longer frozen and unable to go out on stage and try stuff, I became more comfortable doing the thing I was afraid of doing. This familiarity made me less afraid—less, but still afraid.

So, fear is not the problem. The problem is when you let your fear keep you from doing what you want to do.

I will always be a little afraid, and that's okay—because I have courage.

Chapter 9
11 Habits of Highly Successful Improvisers

1. Agreement: Everyone in the scene make-believing the same thing.

It is almost silly to put agreement on the list because it seems so basic. But I can tell you, highly successful improvisers get out of their own way and figure out the basic scenic agreement with their partner and fast. I know everybody wants to get their character's point of view out there, start playing their cool game, and hear the audience laugh after they say something, but that does not matter until you figure out what you're going to make-believe. So, go ahead and agree to whatever it is you are doing.

Let's be honest—doing improv is a high-stress activity for almost everyone who is doing it, and that stress causes humans to get a little agitated. That agitation can make you act like a jerk, and being a jerk makes you want to disagree. Disagreement creates uninteresting conflict because no one knows the context for the argument. Let's go ahead and call that out—watching people argue without knowing why is not fun.

Without the agreement, you are not earning the conflict through some really cool make-believe. You are disagreeing because you have no clue what to do in the scene. You don't know what to do in the scene because you have not filled out your agreement. And it gets worse—that void you are creating, the void of being in a scene without answering the basic question of "What am I trying to make-believe?" makes you more agitated and gets filled up with a bunch of negativity.

Why do improvisers undermine their agreement by saying "no" to each other? Because when you are in the panic of not knowing what you are make-believing, no feels really good. No feels good because when you know nothing about what you are pretending, you feel out of control. You feel out of control because you are out of control, and saying "no" is your attempt to get back in control. That is why it feels so good to play a negative point of view before anything is established in the scene. Saying "no" gets you back in control.

The problem is that in gaining control, you just killed the joy of agreeing to be out of control with your partner. That is what we are agreeing to—collaboration with others to create something that no one person controls.

So, next time you have no clue what to do, try to just agree to the make-believe, hold off on the negativity, and start pretending right away or join in with the other person's make-believe and do a scene together, one line at a time. It might be fun.

2. Being emotionally altered by your scene partner.

Highly successful improvisers are ready and willing to care about what their scene partner does and says. Figuring out the emotional cause and effect between the characters is required for a scene to succeed. If you figure out how your partner emotionally alters you, then you know what to heighten in the scene. Your character's emotional transformation, moment by moment, caused by your scene partner, is how the audience figures out what kind of character you are. It is how we connect to your character and your character's story. It is how we empathize with you. It is how we understand what is going on. So go ahead—be emotionally altered by your scene partner. Feel the powerful rush of an audience seeing themselves in you and hoping your character gets what they want.

Unfortunately, the opposite is also true. If your character is not affected by what happens in the scene, we won't be either. If you don't care, we don't care. And just so you know, being emotionally altered by your scene partner does not mean being angry with your scene partner. Anger is just one color in the emotional rainbow, and we want to see the whole spectrum of emotional colors in your response to your scene partner.

Here is another big advantage to being altered and feeling deeply in response to what your partner is doing and saying: if you know how you feel, you will know what to say. Really, just try it out. Think about something you care deeply about—a prized possession, an important event in your life, a best friend. Now start talking about this person, thing, or event. I'll check back in five minutes.

See, I told you. You probably spent the last five minutes rambling about your person, thing, or event and not once did you run out of stuff to say. I repeat—if you know how you feel, you will know what to say. If you did run out of stuff to say, then pick something you care more about next time.

3. Knowing something about your character—immediately.

When starting scenes, highly successful improvisers figure out something about themselves—fast. They choose to know something specific about their character, and then they do stuff with that knowledge in mind. It does not matter what they figure out about their character—it could be anything—but successful improvisers make a specific choice about their character immediately. Then they play with that knowledge.

You have probably heard this improv mantra before: "How you do what you do is who you are in the scene."

Knowing something specific about your character immediately leads you right to some "how." Highly successful improvisers throw some *how* at what they are doing and then figure it out as they go. For example, if I start a scene as a cab driver and say to my scene partner, "I was glad to get a customer this late at night in this part of town." My partner knows she is the customer in a cab, but what kind of customer is she going to be? Successful improvisers will make a choice immediately about who they are and play a strong "how."

When highly successful improvisers choose to know something about their character, they don't stop at one thing. There are millions of things you can know about your character—their age, their gender, their emotional state—but what's more important is what I refer to as the domino effect. Highly successful improvisers commit to a choice about their character, and that choice has a domino effect leading to other specific choices. The thing you choose to know immediately is important because it leads to a series of discoveries and other choices about who your character is. Highly successful improvisers use the domino effect to go from knowing one thing about their character to knowing everything about their character.

See chapter 16 for step-by-step methods that use the domino effect to go from knowing one thing about your character to knowing everything about your character.

Let's pause for a word about character exaggeration. Lots of the comedy in improvisation comes from playing over-the-top or unbelievable characters. Performers can get so much approval from the audience for an over-the-top character, they bring the same character back over and over again. Some of the most loved characters in comedy were created this way. However, knowing something about yourself at the top of a scene does not have to lead to character exaggeration. You can use the same method to create realistic characters as well. Play with both types of characters. Highly successful improvisers can play realistic characters that are believable, as well as exaggerated characters in a heightened reality.

4. Pantomime: Pretending to touch stuff that is not there.

Improv nerds like to use the term *space work* or *object work*. Well, that just sounds pretentious. Theatre has had a word for pretending to touch stuff that is not there for a couple thousand years—pantomime. Highly successful improvisers do it often and do it well.

They are not magically able to do it because they are talented—they are able to do it because they work at it.

Space work, object work, pantomime—or whatever you call it—separates the adults from the children in improv. If you cannot realistically pretend you are pouring a cup of tea or turning a page in a book, then you can't improvise. You heard me. Two guys just standing on stage insulting each other's sexual prowess might make the morons in the audience laugh, but it ain't improv. If you want to do that, get a microphone and tell some jokes. We are not doing stand-up. We are creating spontaneous theatre without props, scenery, or costumes, so you are going to have to pantomime.

Successful improvisers touch stuff that is not there, and when they do, the audience's imagination fills in the space with the object, and that's cool. Improv is transformation—actors transform into different characters and it is your job to transform the space into different places, which you do with your body by pantomiming. Go practice.

5. Vulnerability: Letting your guard down so you are affected by your world.

Most of the time when I say the word *vulnerability*, people hear the word *weak*. Don't look at it that way. Vulnerability is just letting your guard down, and when you are improvising it is your job to let your guard down. You need to put yourself in a flexible state of being, so stuff that happens during the scene can alter you. We are looking for one character to have an effect on the other character. It is that cause and effect that we want to see in a scene. Being altered by your scene partner is just so much easier to achieve if you let your guard down.

Here's another way of thinking about vulnerability in improv: hope for a positive outcome in a situation where you don't have control.

Let's try to create a little vulnerability, okay? Think of examples from your real life of things that you hope work out well but you have no or limited control of. You should have plenty of real stuff, both positive and negative, to pull from. Stuff like recovering from an injury, asking a person out on a date, or wanting a promotion.

Now, after you find your real-life example, allow yourself to drop into that feeing of vulnerability. Be honest with yourself and make sure it is something you are hoping for, but don't control the outcome. Examine how you feel.

That is your vulnerability.

Now that you know how you feel when you let your guard down, try playing with that feeling in scenes. It can be magic.

It is the combination of letting your guard down and hoping to get what you want that puts the character into a heightened state. We want characters in improv scenes to stay vulnerable in situations that we, in real life, would never remain vulnerable in. Think about all the classic characters from film, television, and plays that are forced to be in this heightened and vulnerable state. Think about every guy in every romantic comedy ever made. You could argue that having a character in a heightened state, hopeful for a positive outcome but not in control, is required to create comedy. So, cultivate your vulnerability to be able to play it in scenes.

To recap, vulnerability means letting your guard down and hoping for a positive outcome. Letting your guard down puts you in a flexible state of being and makes you more likely to be altered by what happens in the scene. Being altered in the scene will move you toward creating a cause-and-effect relationship with your partner. Enter into that cause-and-effect relationship with your partner, and you will know exactly what to do in the scene, how to do it, and why you are doing it. Wouldn't that be fun—knowing the what, how, and why in an improv scene for a change. This might sound easy, but it's hard to do. Why?

Anger.

A word about vulnerability and anger: lots of people (and in my experience, especially men) mistake vulnerability with getting angry with their scene partner and yelling a bunch. Anger is only one (and perhaps a classically masculine one) response to feeling vulnerable. Remember, vulnerability is a character letting their guard down and hoping for a positive outcome without the ability to control said outcome. Anger in response to vulnerability is an attempt to control the outcome. Enter anger, exit vulnerability. It is the balance of hope and lack of control that makes vulnerability beautiful to watch.

6. Trust and Support of your Partner, Group and Team: Trust is confidence that your team will be there for you. Support is being there for your team.

Highly successful improvisers trust that the team will be there for them, no matter what. They know that if they jump, the team will catch them, and because each individual has confidence in the group, the group has confidence in itself.

Highly successful improvisers are there for their team, no matter what. That is what support is—everyone being there for everyone else, regardless of anything. The key to supporting others is doing it immediately. If something is needed, just give it. Most people wait until they understand what is going on before they jump out there. Waiting until you understand before you jump out there is not support—it is judgment. If you wait until you know what is going on, most of the time, the moment where support was needed has passed. Support is all about just being there for the other guy. Even if you have no clue as to what is going on—especially when you have no clue what is going on.

Be there for each other, and have confidence they will be there for you.

The hard part is that you can't fake trust. When someone does not trust you, you can smell that judgment a mile away. And when someone does not trust you, then you don't trust them.

It gets worse.

Without trust, you can't support. Think about it—what exactly are you trusting the other guy to do? You are trusting them to be there for you when you need their support. Support creates trust, and trust is required to support. Trust and support are in a cause-and-effect relationship. If you trust me, I trust you. If you don't, I don't. If you support me, then I support you. If you don't, I don't.

Heavy stuff, but the good news is that you can cultivate trust.

Trust is born from taking the risk to communicate honestly. Highly successful improvisers trust their group enough to risk being honest with them. They communicate their expectations for rehearsals and performance, honestly. Through this honest communication, the group can discover common goals and methods and start trusting each other.

If you want to trust someone you are working with, talk to them. Discuss what you want out of the work. Listen to what they want. Find your common ground and constantly reevaluate based on your process. If you are honest in your communication and have common goals and methods, then you will trust everyone is doing the work for the same reason. This works. Trust me.

7. Specificity: Seeing, touching, and talking about your make-believe world in detail.

Highly successful improvisers constantly work toward the specific in their make-believe. They are not satisfied with anything vague or fuzzy when it comes to the five scenic elements. Improv hates a vacuum, and highly successful improvisers fill that void with specific choices about their make-believe scene. When they pantomime opening a door, it is not to a "room"—it is to the "laundry room." When they react emotionally to their scene partner, they aren't "happy"—they are "happy their wife got home early from work." Highly successful improvisers are addicted to being specific with everything they offer on stage.

When it comes to specificity, highly successful improvisers do two things. First, they push their experience of the make-believe to the specific, and second, they share that specificity with their scene partner. It's hard work and takes practice, but every time you experience and share a specific detail about your make-believe, you strengthen the reality of the scene.

Highly successful improvisers do not limit themselves to being specific with facts. Being specific is not about trivia—knowing what year the Franco-Prussian War was fought is all well and good—but being specific is about more than just listing information. Being specific is not an end or a destination; it is a means to get to where you want to go. The goal is to create a real world with specific details that you can connect with emotionally. The specific details help the improviser believe in their world and care about the people and stuff in that world. Humans need details to become invested, so it is natural that if you know nothing about a person, place, or thing, you would not care about that person, place, or thing. Remember, if you don't care, then we don't care, so add details with specificity like crazy, but remember the goal. The goal is not to add specific details to prove you're intelligent; it's to add details to increase your investment in the make-believe. The details should make the pretend world more real for you.

8. Commitment: Having the guts to stick with your choices even when they aren't working.

Highly successful improvisers commit to their choices. They leave their self-consciousness and judgment behind and just do whatever needs to be done. When an improviser truly commits, they won't change their strategy, even if all signs point to failure. They go all in. They dive head first into the scene before they even know what's going on.

If they make a choice, they stick with it for the duration of the scene. Whatever they do, they do completely. If they choose to be a talking tree that is sad that his/her apples are getting picked, then they commit to that reality, even if that reality is ridiculous—especially if that reality is ridiculous.

In improv scene work, commitment creates reality and reality increases commitment. If you commit to your choices, you will create a reality, and if you buy into that reality, you will increase your commitment.

When improvisers don't commit to their own choices, it's like they are doing the scene halfway, and doing improv halfway makes the whole thing kind of silly. You can't make-believe halfway.

Why do improvisers lack commitment to their choices? Judgment.

Improvisers bail on their own choices when they judge themselves or the scene as failing. As improvisers, we have to kick this addiction to success. We need some good old-fashioned failure to learn how to be okay with it. So, when failure starts to show up, we won't run away and bail on our choices—we will dig in and commit.

That's what commitment means—doing something even when it is failing.

Highly successful improvisers just make a choice and then they go there. They commit to the given circumstance, to their character's point of view, to the reality, and then they just play in that world.

9. Honesty: Tell the truth and we will believe you.

Highly successful improvisers gain the audience's trust by saying what they mean and meaning what they say. Tell the truth and we will believe you. We'll believe you and then start to care about what happens to your character. If the audience cares about what happens to your character, everything gets so much easier. If the audience cares, they can believe in you, as well as laugh at you. You start to get a whole new way to measure success for your work. Work honestly, and the audience will respond with hope, shock, fear, and laughter—the whole spectrum of emotion when watching honest human behavior.

If you reveal your truth, the audience will believe you and immediately form a bond with you. The audience will empathize with you and see themselves in your actions. Highly successful improvisers form this bond with the audience and exploit it for all it is worth.

Honesty, empathy, truth—wait a minute, that doesn't sound like comedy. That sounds like actor speak. Exactly. That is what you are doing in an improv scene—you are acting. You are trying to get the people who are sitting in the dark watching you pretend to drive a car to believe you are driving a car, and it is just so much easier if you believe you are driving a car. That starts with simple honesty.

10. Mischief: misbehaving in a good-natured, playful way.

Highly successful improvisers misbehave, and we love to watch. A way to create some mischief is to figure out what you are not supposed to do in a scene and then do that. Do that thing that you are not supposed to do over and over again. Misbehave all over the place, but be sure to do it in a way that makes us like you. How do you do that? Make sure the bad behavior is good-natured. Enjoy your bad behavior and feel sorry for the havoc you create—just make sure you keep doing the mischief.

Here is the flip side of the coin—highly successful improvisers also recognize mischief. Work to be skilled in both positions. Yes, it is fun to be the crazy wife at the office party, but we also need the sane husband who is afraid he will lose his job if his wife gets too crazy. But remember, a little goes a long way when it comes to complaining about your scene partner's behavior. Think about it. Do we want to see the crazy wife do lots of specific mischief at the office party, or do we want to watch the husband complain about it? We want the mischief, but we need a little complaint to be able to recognize the behavior of the wife as mischief.

So go ahead and misbehave—break the flowerpot, say the inappropriate thing—just do it playfully. Then do it again. Whatever you do, keep doing the mischief, even if there is a guy complaining about the mischief trying to stop you. Many times, a character will create an awesome piece of mischief, and then their scene partner freaks out on them for doing the mischief. Then the person doing the mischief feels bad for being playful and stops doing the mischief and then the scene tanks.

Start mischievous—stay playful.

11. Reincorporation: Bringing specific stuff back from earlier in the show, piece or scene.

Highly successful improvisers bring stuff back. They reincorporate. They call back. Basically, they repeat stuff. Why? Because it's funny, because it makes the earlier stuff seem important rather than random, because it makes the show as a whole mean something—but honestly, mostly because it is funny. Highly successful improvisers look backwards, not forwards. They don't worry about what comes next—they remember what came before. They remember what they did earlier and what impact it had. Then they repeat the behavior, looking for that same response.

Repeating stuff is important both in scene work and in creating connections among scenes. In scene work, if touching dad's just-washed car made him freak out, repeat the behavior—dad will freak out again. Good for you; you just heightened dad's point of view. You repeated the behavior that caused the tension to increase. If you are doing a long form, and three scenes ago, you touched dad's just-washed car and he freaked out, edit and start a new scene where you are touching something that you shouldn't be touching and your scene partner (if they are highly successful) will repeat the heightened behavior. Everyone looks like a genius.

Highly successful improvisers remember what they do and the effect it had, and they look for opportunities to repeat that behavior in the scene and in the piece.

Chapter 10
Read This Before You Start Doing the Exercises

Before we jump head first into a bunch of improv exercises, I want to mention a phenomenon I have seen occur in some students when faced with all my little systems, step-by-step methods, and philosophies: they shut down—creatively.

Now, it's my hope that this book will help you enjoy doing improv even more than you already do. Furthermore, I hope the ideas and exercises in this book will help your entire group get to where they want to go with improv. But not every improviser is going to want to approach improv in the way that is outlined in these pages.

Some improvisers are going to get creatively shut down by all this technical information about scenic elements, structure, and so forth. This heavy-conscious thought about improv will put them "in their head." Making choices based on technique will cause these improvisers to feel uninspired and, therefore, kill the fun and spontaneity for them. They will not want to do the exercises outlined in next few chapters because these exercises will dictate some of the choices they have to make. It is natural to resist change, so encourage these improvisers to work outside of their comfort zone for a while. Usually, with enough encouragement or peer pressure, they will at least try some of the exercises, and really, that's all I am asking for—a good honest try.

But sometimes you will work with an improviser who just does not want to try new things. This improviser has found a way that works for him, and he is uninterested in learning new ways of doing what he thinks he already knows how to do. If this improviser does not respond to the group's encouragement to try something new, then get him out of the room *right now*. Get him out of there and surround yourself with people who want to do these exercises.

And while you're at it, consider getting the most "talented" person out of the room as well. Seriously, if you have a person in your group who is really good in performance but is constantly complaining about doing this highly technical work in rehearsal, get them out of the room now.

Why?

Because the most talented member of a group is the least interested in developing techniques that make the group better as a whole. Here's why: a highly technical, step-by-step approach will not make talented people better. It will make hard-working people who want to seem talented better. Often, the most talented person in your group does not want the rest of the group to learn new step-by-step methods to seem really talented.

Why?

Because the new step-by-step methods will make the most talented person in the group look less talented by reducing the perceived talent gap between the players. In other words, you will get better by using these step-by-step methods and they will not, so that most talented person won't seem most talented anymore. If someone is complaining about trying something new because their regular modus operandi is working so well for them, get them out of there. They are making choices based on their own need to be seen as the best. Instead, surround yourself with people who want to learn how to make everyone in the group look good.

How do these exercises and step-by-step methods make

everyone look good?

The exercises will train you to make the step-by-step methods automatic. We make the step-by-step methods automatic so that we can establish concrete beginnings of scenes in which everyone knows what they are make-believing. If everyone knows what to make-believe, then everyone is going to be much more comfortable doing improvisation. The most talented person on your team does not want you comfortable—he wants you nervous so he can shine the next time he is in a scene with you.

This most talented person may also be reluctant to warm-up before shows. He may sabotage exercises and undermine group focus. Why? Because he wants you cold, unskilled, and unfocused so you make him look better. This person sees cooperation and technique as obstacles to him shining in scenes.

I suggest making sure everyone participating in the exercises is honestly open-minded to trying new things.

As you work on the exercises, set a goal for your entire group to make the step-by-step methods outlined in this book automatic, so you automatically know how to build an agreement with your partner by establishing the five scenic elements. So, without even having to think about it, you know how to explore your character point of view to discover your Primary Emotional Drive. And, because you have practiced it so many times, you know how to repeat and intensify cause and effect and raise the stakes to heighten a scene. When these methods become automatic, the technique will support your creativity, and everyone in your group will share the same basic skill set.

Now it's time for the exercises.

Chapter 11
What to Do, Step by Step, to Create Awesome Scenes

On page 6 of this book, I made the following claim: "This book will teach what to do, step by step, to create awesome scenes."

Wow, talk about ego.

Well, here we go. It's time for me to put my money where my mouth is. Now is when I'm supposed to outline my methodology. So, here's what I am going to do. In the following chapters I am going to go though the steps that I think are necessary in order to create great scenes. For each step I will give you exercises and methods that will help you learn how to do that step. These exercises and methods work for me. They are not theoretical; these methods are exactly what I do when I improvise. That is what I am going to give you with these exercises—literally—how I do improv.

I just teach what I do when I improvise, and if it works for me, I think it can work for just about anybody.

So the following chapters are what I do, step by step, to create awesome scenes.

Note about these exercises and methods: Most of these exercises and methods are designed for groups, so go find some like-minded people to play with. Also, I describe the exercises and step-by-step methods with a facilitator in mind, so it will be helpful to assign a person to take the group through each exercise. Try to change this person up every few exercises or they will become your de facto director, which is cool if you like that sort of thing.

Chapter 12
Step 1:
Getting Connected

Your first step in creating awesome scenes is to get everyone who is going to be doing the improvisation connected. How do I get everyone connected? I get the group to play silly games that force them to cooperate with each other. The problem is that most humans are pretty bad at cooperating.

Why?

Because people are self-conscious, they are worried about themselves. And I have some news for you, while you are being self-conscious you are focusing on yourself—you are self-focused. Here's the problem with that: While you are self-focused, you are not connected with your partner or group. If everyone in the group is self-focused, then no one is connected.

I have found that the easiest way to get connected and stop being worried about yourself is to focus on someone else; this is called other-focus. While you are focused on "other," you are not worrying about "self," you are connecting with your partner. That's what other-focus creates—connection.

So here is how it goes: in order to connect with your partner or group you have to learn how to create other-focus. The following exercise will help you do just that; it is the first exercise I do in every class I ever teach. It will help you get connected with your partner or group by developing the skill of consciously shifting your focus from self to other.

The First Exercise: The Focus Push-up

People spend most of their time focused on themselves. It's natural to do this, but for improv, your self-focus has to be balanced with taking in the stuff that is happening around you. Think about it—have you ever heard this: "Bob is such an awesome improviser; he is always so focused on himself." No, you have never heard that, because nobody ever says it. If Bob is all about himself, then he's no fun to play with.

Too much self-focus creates either self-judgment or ego, and both get in the way of successful group improvisation. The self-judging people are worried if other people like them, and the egotists don't care. I want to do improv with people who care about how the group sees them but are not worried if they are liked. How do you become one of these people in the sweet spot—caring about the group, but not losing your individuality? You balance self-focus with other-focus.

No kidding. Balancing self-focus with other-focus works like magic to get rid of the ill effects of too much self-focus. If you are balancing these two points of focus (other and self), you are constantly checking in with your partner, and therefore, what you think, feel, and do will be based on what you are getting from them. Hey, that sounds a lot like listening to me.

I start every workshop I ever teach with the following exercise. This exercise helps develop the skill of consciously shifting your focus from self to other. I call it the Focus Push-up.

THE FOCUS PUSH-UP ROUND ONE: EYE CONTACT

Step 1.
Get everyone in a circle.

Step 2.
Have everyone shake his/her hands. Yes, just have everyone simply shake their hands around a bunch, like they might be warming up for some kind of physical activity. The hand-shaking thing is just a simple physical activity that takes everyone out of their heads and into their bodies. While they are doing this physical hand-shaking thing, have everyone make eye contact.

So, to repeat, shake your hands around and make eye contact with the other people in the circle who are also shaking their hands.

This eye contact is an example of other-focus. Remind everyone that it is possible to enjoy eye contact. This will make most people smile at each other, and that can't hurt.

Step 3.
After a few seconds of everyone shaking his/her hands and making eye contact, have everyone in the circle shift from other-focus to self-focus. I prompt the focus shift by calling out a body part that is not the hands, like the head or shoulders. When I call out this other body part, I tell everyone to move this body part and shift from other-focus to internal or self-focus. So, while they move this body part, they are self-focused, and while they are shaking their hands and making eye contact they are other-focused.

Step 4.
Repeat this "other" to "self" focus shift.

Here is the order I use:

1. Shake hands with eye contact and other-focus.

2. Shift the movement to the head with eyes closed and self-focus.

3. Shift the movement back to the hands with eye contact and other-focus.

4. Shift the movement to the shoulders with eyes closed and self-focus.

5. Shift the movement back to the hands with eye contact and other-focus.

6. Shift the movement to the ribs with eyes closed and self-focus.

7. Shift the movement back to the hands with eye contact and other-focus.

8. Shift the movement to the hips with eyes closed and self-focus.

9. Shift the movement back to the hands with eye contact and other-focus.

10. Shift the movement to the knees with eyes closed and self-focus.

11. Shift the movement back to the hands with eye contact and other-focus.

12. Shift the movement to the feet with eyes closed and self-focus.

I call this a "focus push-up" because it isolates the effort it takes to manipulate your focus from self to other and back again. This natural focus shift is required to listen and *yes and* information. While we are other-focused, we are making eye contact, harvesting information, and becoming aware of what is being created around us. While we are self-focused, we are thinking about the eye contact we just had and processing the information we harvested while we were other-focused.

It is kind of like breathing. You breathe in the air around you, and when you take it in, you pull out the stuff you need to use to stay alive. Other-focus is breathing in what your partner is doing, and self-focus is taking the stuff you breathed in and processing it into your point of view.

THE FOCUS PUSH-UP ROUND TWO: HARVEST ONE PIECE OF INFORMATION

Now repeat the exercise, but this time, while everyone is shaking their hands with other-focus, instead of having them just make eye contact, have them "harvest one piece of information from the group with their eyes." This means that, instead of only making eye contact with the other people in the group, they can look at all the parts of other people's bodies. While they shake their hands, they can harvest the type of clothes someone is wearing, their eye color, their expression—whatever piece of specific information they want.

During round two, when you prompt the group to shift from other-focus to self-focus, tell them to keep their eyes closed and think about the piece of information that they just harvested.

Here is how I prompt the group during round two:

"Shake your hands with other-focus and harvest one piece of specific information from the group. It could be anything; like John is wearing a blue polo shirt or Jessica has on silver earrings. Now, after you harvest, shift to self-focus, close your eyes, and move your head around. Roll your head forward and side-to-side. While you move your head in self-focus, think about the piece of information you just harvested. Focus on the body part you are moving and the information you just harvested. Take that information into your body."

I repeat this process for each body part, getting the players to harvest a different piece of information every time they are other-focused and shaking their hands.

After we complete the round, I ask each player to tell the group one piece of information they harvested during the exercise. This helps them get comfortable making specific observations about each other, which is good for scene work.

THE FOCUS PUSH-UP ROUND THREE: HARVEST AND ASSOCIATE

For round three, you repeat all the steps from round two, but now you do something with the pieces of information you harvest.

Now, when you shift to self-focus and think about the piece of information you harvested, allow yourself to associate with the information.

For example, let's say you saw a silvery belt buckle while you were other-focused; when you shift to internal or self-focus, think about that belt buckle.

Ask yourself the question, "What does that silvery belt buckle make me think, feel, or remember?" Maybe it makes you think of werewolves because it's silver or of a rodeo because it's a belt buckle or of your dad's chest-of-drawers because he used to put his belts there. Whatever the answer to that question is (and it could be anything; it does not matter), that is your association to the silvery belt buckle that you harvested.

That is what we are trying to do with this exercise—harvest specific information and figure out what it means to us.

Here are the steps you take in round three to associate:

- Shake hands with other-focus.
- Harvest one specific piece of information from the group.
- Shift movement to other body part.
- Shift focus to self-focus.
- Associate or ask yourself what does the information I harvested make me think, feel, or remember.

After round three is complete, have everyone in the circle share one thing they harvested and what that thing made them think, feel, or remember.

The goal of round three of the focus push-up is to teach the following step-by-step process:

Step 1: Focus on other
Step 2: Harvest specific information
Step 3: Shift focus to the self
Step 4: Internalize the information
Step 5: Associate to figure out what this information means to you

These five steps are the same ones you follow during good improv scene work. You take in information and process it into a response. You have to learn how to manipulate your focus so you can place it wherever in needs to be at any moment in the scene. When your partner is making an offer, use other-focus to harvest information. After you get the information, use self-focus to process that information and figure out what it means to you so you can respond. Your response is a combination of what you got from your partner during other-focus and how what you got made you feel during self-focus.

That is how I know what to do and say in an improv scene. I use the harvest-internalize-associate process to listen and respond when I'm in a scene. If you master the harvest-internalize-associate process, you will always know what to do or say in a scene. This process is how we can live moment by moment in the scenes that we create. It is how we can support our partner. It is how we *yes and*.

More Exercises to Get Connected

You have done the focus push-up, and your group is learning how to harvest information using other-focus. You are learning to take the information you harvest and process it into your response.

For me, that is how I connect with my partner or group. I get something from my partner—I call that harvesting—and then I react. But I don't react randomly; I react based on that thing I got from my partner—I call that associating. I base what I do on what I get from my partner; I harvest, associate, and then react. That is how I know we are connected.

This process of switching from harvesting in other-focus to associating in self-focus is just like scene work, because when the other guy is doing anything—pantomiming, talking, whatever—I am other-focused. I am harvesting information that the other person is creating by what they are doing and saying. I take that into myself, and I figure out what that means to me and that informs my response.

So if I am other-focused when my partner is making offers and my partner is other-focused when I am making offers, then what we do and say is going to make a lot more sense. But if I am self-focused while my partner is making an offer, nervous about the scene going well, or thinking about what I am going to say, then what I do is not going to have any connection to what I am being given by my partner. How can it? I did not hear or see what my partner did. I couldn't, because I was not other-focused.

This shifting of focus from self to other is the effort of cooperation. It is the process of scene work and makes sure that what I do is dealing with what was just said.

Here are some games and exercises that further cultivate the other/self-focus shift and force everyone in the group to base what they do on what they get from someone else. And when everyone agrees to base what they do on what they get, then we have some group cooperation.

CLAP WALK/CLAP STOP

Have everyone stand in the playing area, and make sure the space is safe to move around in. The teacher claps, and everyone walks. The teacher claps again, and everyone stops. Follow the pattern of "clap walk, clap stop" until the group gets good at starting and stopping. Now tell the group that anyone can clap. The group now leads itself, but make sure every clap is heard by the group. If two people clap, they cancel each other out. If someone does all the clapping, tell him or her to try not to lead the group.

After the group gets good at self-leading starting and stopping, see if they can do it without clapping.

Side Coaching:
"That was two claps, so you start and stop."
"Keep your focus on the group."

GIVE AND TAKE

Have everyone form a circle, and two players enter the circle. Only one player can move at a time, but someone must always be moving. So, if one player is moving and another player starts to move, then the player who was moving must stop. You can "give" the movement to your partner by stopping, or they can "take" the movement by starting. If a player only gives or only takes, ask them to try the one they have not done. Try it with three or more players. Add nonverbal sound to the movement.

Side Coaching:
"If he starts to move, you have to stop."
"Stop moving the moment you see the other person start."
"Try giving, as well as taking."

KNIFE, BABY, ANGRY CAT

In a circle, one person pantomimes throwing a knife at another person. The person throwing makes a "ninja sound" when they throw the knife, and the person catching makes the same noise when they catch the knife. Make sure the players are engaged in eye contact.

After the group gets good at throwing and catching the knife, add a pantomimed baby to throw and catch in the circle. Give the baby size and a little baby voice, and throw it the way you would toss a fragile baby.

After they can handle the knife and the baby, add a pantomimed angry cat to throw and catch around the circle. The cat needs to sound different than the baby. Have all three things being passed at the same time. If someone does not see that you have passed them something, then pass it again with more energy. If the group gets bored of the game, add a new pantomimed object.

Side Coaching:
"Make eye contact before you throw."
"Make it clear where you are throwing the knife."
"Pick your target before you throw."

PASS THE CLAP

Once again, have everyone stand in a circle, and one person makes eye contact with another person in the circle. The two people who are looking at each other then clap at the same time. The person who was sent the clap now sends the clap to another person by making eye contact and clapping at the same time as that person. The goal is not to clap as fast as you can, the goal is to establish a rhythm and for people to really make connections with fellow ensemble members. Try walking around while you do it.

Side Coaching:
"It is not about going fast—it's about going together."
"Heighten your need to send, and heighten your need to receive."

YES—YOU

Everyone forms a circle, and one person points to another. The person being pointed at says the word *yes*. After that person says *yes*, and only after, the person who was pointing gets to walk toward the person who said *yes* and rejoin the circle. Now the person who said *yes* points to another person, and that person must say *yes*, giving the person who pointed permission to walk toward them. Make sure people are waiting for the *yes*. Do it with two people at a time. Then do it with three people at a time. Do it with only eye contact and no speaking.

I usually warn groups that have never played this game that it is going to be frustrating for about three minutes, and then it is going to become very easy. This helps them work through the frustration.

Side Coaching:
"Wait for the yes before you go."
"There are two types of people: those who wait for the *yes* before they go, and those who don't. The ones who don't wait are not basing what they do on what they are getting from their partner."

THE JOIN DRILL

See chapter 4.

ONE-WORD STORIES

With everyone in a circle, tell the group you are going to create a story together. The story is going to be told in third-person narrative, so the players won't use the words *I*, *me*, or *my*. You tell the group that you will handle the sentence structure by saying, "Period, new sentence." You start the story by saying, "Once upon a time . . ." then each person in the group adds one word at a time. Go in order around the circle, and stop when the story no longer makes sense. Try two words at a time. Then try three words at a time.

Side Coaching:
"Try to create short, simple sentences."
"Keep it narrative, and stay away from dialogue."

CONDUCTED STORY

Get two to eight players in a line, shoulder to shoulder—yes, actually touching shoulders. Tell the group you are going to create a story together. The story is going to be told in third-person narrative, so the players won't use the words *I*, *me*, or *my*. I give the players the title of a story that has never been told. When the conductor points at a player, they narrate the story. When the conductor cuts them off, they must stop. The conductor changes the storyteller often and quickly, allowing one player to start a sentence and another to finish it.

Side Coaching:
"A story has a character who encounters a challenge, and then that character either does or does not overcome the challenge."
"If the title is *The Little Boy Who Could Fly*, then the story should probably have a boy who can fly in it."
"Pick up right where he left off."
"Finish her sentence."
"If you start a sequence of dialogue, then it eventually needs to end."

When you play these games with your group, encourage the development of these skills:

- Shifting from self-focus to other-focus
- Basing what you do on what you got from your partner
- Basing what you say on the last thing said
- Realistic pantomime

Chapter 13
Step 2
Yes and . . .

By now, your group is connected. Each player is able to focus on another player and harvest information. The next step to creating awesome scenes is to start *yes and*-ing the information you harvest from your partner.

Here is how I defined *yes and* . . . earlier in the book:

> *Yes and* . . . is the process of taking whatever your partner gives you, agreeing to it (that's the *yes* part), and then adding more to it (that's the *and* part). In a scene, when a player moves or speaks, they are creating specific information about their world. Then that information is *yes and*-ed—it is agreed to and added to. It is this basic back and forth between players, this agreeing and adding, that allows for spontaneous collaboration.

The first thing you need to do when you *yes and* is see what your partner is offering, and that requires other-focus. When I am other-focused and harvesting information, I am not doing it to be a good listener—I am doing it so I can respond in a way that makes sense. You can't *yes and* with any random response—you need the thing you add to connect with what you were given. You need to base what you give on what you get.

These exercises will give you some experience with *yes and*. They will help you learn how to harvest information, agree with what you harvested, and then add something based on what you got.

Exercises

Remember, as the first exercise below illustrates, you *yes and* with your body, as well as your words. I put these exercises in the order that I feel works best.

"HEY, CATCH THIS BABY!"

In this game, you are going to pantomime throwing and catching pantomimed objects, so get everyone in a circle. One person in the circle throws a pantomimed object at another person in the circle. When they throw the object they say, "Hey, catch this (name of object)!" The object can be anything at all. The person catching the object has to accept what they are being thrown and catch it the way they would if the object was real. Then the person who caught the object throws a different object at someone else in the circle. This exercise gets players to make specific offers and physically accept what they are given by their partner. Catching what the other players throw at you teaches you to physically *yes and* each other's ideas.

Side Coaching:
"Catch that baby as if it were a real baby."
"Throw stuff that is hard to catch."

EXPERT CIRCLE

With everyone in a circle, have one person step into the center. The people on the edge of the circle ask the person in the middle open-ended questions. The person in the center answers the questions with made-up, plausible answers. While the expert is answering the question, he is interrupted by another player asking him another question that he must answer. The players in the circle never let the expert complete an answer. Remember to be nice to the expert—it is not an interrogation.

Here are a couple tips regarding the questions: this game is not about trying to stump the expert; it's about giving the expert the opportunity to share information. Try to ask the expert questions that don't have specific answers. "What is the square root of 16,254?" is not a great question in this game because it has one right answer. "Why did my last girlfriend break up with me?" is a great question because there is no easy answer.

Also, here are some tips about answers: no jokey answers. Stay away from answers that seem to come from another reality. The person must try to sound like they know what they're talking about. If you know the answer to the question, just say it. Try to give answers that are honest and plausible. Offer answers that contain specific information.

Side Coaching:
"Interrupt the expert before he finishes his answer."
"The expert needs to elaborate more with his answers."
"Ask more open-ended questions."
"Everyone should be asking questions."

WE ARE _____.
YES AND _____.

Once again, everyone stands in a circle. One at a time, players introduce themselves and the person to their right as a pair of characters. When a player introduces his/her self and the player to their right, they use this line: "We are _____," and they fill in the blank with any type of character. Here are some examples:

"We are cowboys."
"We are two trees that can talk."
"We are on our first date."

Then the person to the right of the player that spoke first says, "Yes, and we _____," filling in the blank with something that makes sense based on what they received. Here is an example:

Player 1: "We are cowboys."
Player 2: "Yes, and we love our horses."

Everyone rewards the pair with a short round of applause. Then the player who said "Yes, and . . ." gets to introduce a new pair of characters. Repeat the pattern until everyone in the circle has a turn.

A few tips to keep in mind with this game: no famous people; you are not doing impersonations—you are doing characters. Encourage the players to physically and vocally transform into the character they are assigned.

Side Coaching:
"Transform your body into the character you were just given."
"*Yes and* with your body and voice."

THE JOIN DRILL: CONCRETE

See page 40.

YES AND IN CHAIRS

Two players sit in chairs. One of the players makes what I call a *we* statement, like, "We robbed a bank this past weekend," or "We just got married." Then the other player says, "Yes, and . . ." then adds some new information. The players take turns speaking, always starting their line with, "Yes, and . . ." These characters are speaking directly to the audience.

It is very important that the players deal with the last thing said. For example, if the first statement was "We robbed a bank this past weekend," and the other player responded by saying, "Yes, and I like popsicles," then I would say that player is not really dealing with what they were given. Look for the players to physically transform into character, or, as I say, *yes and* with your body as well as your words.

This game will expose people who are inherently negative in their choices. Some players have a really hard time *yes and*-ing their partner. Their first response to any offer always seems to be *yes but*. *Yes and* is learned behavior, and if you or a member of your team has a problem *yes and*-ing, then play this game until it becomes automatic.

Side Coaching:
"Deal with the last thing said."
"*Yes and* with specific details."
"You are saying *yes but*—this game is called *yes and*."

YES AND ENVIRONMENT BUILD

This game can be played in groups or pairs. Give the group a location or environment such as a bakery or train station. Then, one at a time, have players describe the stuff that is in that place. The first player might say, "Right here, there is a huge industrial oven with bread baking in it," then the next player might say, "Yes, and over here we have a wooden table with a dozen loaves of pumpernickel cooling off before being bagged up." Players keep *yes and*-ing the description of the environment until the picture is complete. If you want to, you can have two players do a scene in the fully described environment. Make sure they honor all the stuff that was described.

Side Coaching:
"Be more specific with your description."
"What can you assume about the location by what has already been established?"
"How old is the couch? What color is the car? What can you see through the window?"

THE AD GAME

This game works for groups of three to six players. These players are a marketing team for a new, made-up product. Offer the players a suggestion of a product that is completely absurd, such as a piñata made of sharks or a jet pack for hamburgers. The team must come up with the marketing campaign for this absurd, fabricated product. The key is that after every statement, the whole team must yell, "Yes!" Then the next speaker must say, "Yes, and . . ." then add the new information.

A couple of tips to keep in mind: enthusiasm is important, so yell, "Yes!" after everything said. When a player makes an offer, stay with their idea for a little while and build onto it. Respond to the last thing said. Describe the website, the commercial, and the slogan.

Side Coaching:
"Get excited about each other's ideas."
"Make eye contact. High five each other."

Chapter 14
Step 3
The Pre-scene: The Five-Step Method and the Join

Your group is connected, and they are *yes and*-ing each other—now it is time to start doing scenes. I have found that there are two basic ways to do improv scenes: with some kind of input as inspiration and without any kind of input. Both are perfectly legitimate ways to do improv scenes.

That being said, I do improv scenes by getting input, and that is what I teach.

Most of the time when I teach, I give the improvisers a word as inspiration for their scenes. I provide a word for the group, and then they do a scene. The problem with giving improvisers a word as inspiration is that they think the scene is about the word rather than inspired by the word.

For example, here is what you usually get—if you give improvisers the word *butterfly* to inspire a scene, more often than not, the players will start the scene by saying some variation of these three things:

"I love butterflies."
"I hate butterflies."
"I'm a big butterfly."

Really, you might think I am trying to be funny, but I'm not. I am being completely honest.

The players are literally fixated on the idea of a butterfly and can think of nothing else. It makes sense that they would fixate on the word *butterfly* because they are walking into a void on stage and that is the only thing they were given. So, they hold onto it for dear life. These scenes often fail because they treat the input word as an obligation rather than as an inspiration.

To counteract the "I love (blank), I hate (blank), I'm a big (blank)" phenomenon, I have created a little time and space for the improviser to relax, deal with the input word, and get inspired. I call this time and space *the pre-scene*. The pre-scene is the time and space the improvisers use to transform into character and transport into the world of the scene. During the pre-scene, the players use a technique I call *the five-step method* to start an improv scene. This five-step method processes the word I give as inspiration into a physical offer, and then that offer is joined (pages 34–45) by another player.

Since you already know about the Join, let's take a look at the five-step method.

The five-step method is a way to process any input word into a scenic offer. This method empowers the improviser's imagination and frees them up to start the scene with a strong physical offer based on their own associations with the input word. The five-step method takes the focus off the input word and focuses it on the improviser's response to the word.

Here are the five steps:

Step 1: Input
Step 2: Cascade
Step 3: Selection
Step 4: Specification
Step 5: Manifestation

Let's take a look at each step in depth.

Step 1: Input

Someone says a word aloud. It could be anyone—the audience, a coach, a member of the team. The members of the group take the word in and allow themselves to use the word to create associations.

Step 2: Cascade

In reaction to the input word, the improvisers enter into a free association or cascade of images, emotions, and memories. Anything is legal during the cascade, so don't judge yourself, even if your cascade has nothing to do with the word given to you. Indulge your cascade.

Ask yourself: what does the input word make you think, feel, and remember?

Make sure your cascade includes more than just thoughts and images; work toward sense memories and memories of experiences. For example, if the input word *butterfly* makes you think of your mom coming home from work because she used to wear a dress with a butterfly print, that is totally fine. The key is that you process the input word into your personal response. The images, memories, and emotions that are part of your cascade are more real than just the concept of the input word. Leave the input word behind, and indulge your cascade.

A cascade should have lots of images, emotions, and memories to choose from, so just let yourself go and free associate.

Step 3: Selection

Okay, you have a cascade of images, emotions, and memories flowing through your body. Because you were wide open and nonjudgmental during your cascade, you have lots of stuff to choose from—this is the opposite of being fixated on the input word.

Now select one thing from your cascade to focus on. Select whatever you want; it could be a visualization of a place you have never been, a memory from your childhood, or the sound your alarm clock makes every morning. There are no right or wrong things to pick—just pick whatever seems interesting to you.

Step 4: Specification

After you make your selection, work to create as much detail as you can for your image, emotion, or memory. Try to feel, see, hear, touch, taste, and smell the thing you selected.

Now that you have created some detail for what you selected, focus your selection down to one specific object, sensation, or person. If your detailed memory is a visualization of your first car, then focus down to the furry dice hanging from the rearview mirror, the sensation of driving by yourself for the first time, or the look in your dad's eyes when he gave you the keys.

Narrow your selection down into one specific object, sensation, or person.

Step 5: Manifestation

It's time to do something with your body to start the scene. You have processed the input into a specific object, sensation, or person. To start the scene, all you have to do is manifest with your body any aspect of your specific object, sensation, or person.

You can manifest the object literally by touching it or using it in some way. You could manifest the sensation by playing a character experiencing the sensation. You could manifest the person by playing a character that is like the person you imagined or remembered. There are millions of ways to manifest the specific thing you focused on in your cascade. All that matters is that you are inspired by your cascade to get up out of your chair and do something specific with your body to start the scene.

The thing you do with your body to manifest your selection is what I call an *initial physical offer*. So, during step 5, one player gets up on stage and makes an initial physical offer.

That initial physical offer is joined by another player.
Then the scene starts.

You can use the five-step method to take any input word and process it into an initial physical offer to start a scene. But remember, you are not planning the scene—you are just starting with something specific based on your associations with the input word. Using the five-step method to get to a specific initial offer is just the first half of the pre-scene. The other half of the pre-scene is your partner joining you. The initial physical offer and the Join transforms the players into their characters and transports them to the world of the scene.

Every scene starts with an initial physical offer and a join.

So, when you make your initial physical offer, you wait for a moment before you start the scene. You hold and wait to be joined before you start.

Why?

Because even though you have a rich and detailed memory going on in your mind and you are making a super-specific initial offer to start the scene, you don't own the scene. You don't know how your offer will be joined or *yes and*-ed. Your partner could easily *yes and* you in a way that alters what you thought you were creating.

The pre-scene, or the transformation into a scene, has a first half and a second half. The first half is a player using the five-step method to inspire an initial physical offer—I call this person *the beginner*. The second half of the pre-scene is another player using the Join to somehow connect with the beginner; I call this person *the joiner*.

When a player takes the time and space to make an initial physical offer based on the five-step method, and then another player uses the Join to connect to that offer, they spontaneously define scenic elements. They are defining scenic elements and filling the void most improvisers feel when they walk on stage. And filling that void with scenic elements feels good because it helps players know what to make-believe.

Hello, pre-scene—goodbye, void.

Exercises

The first few times you try to do the five-step method, it will feel like walking through mud. You will think, "How is this supposed to feel spontaneous?" But by the tenth time you do the five steps, you will start to realize the steps are pretty much how your mind works anyway. Soon enough, you'll be able to do the five steps and manifest your initial offer faster than an untrained improviser can say, "I am a big butterfly."

Here are some exercises to help practice following the five steps. I suggest doing these exercises until they become automatic.

TALK THROUGH THE FIVE-STEP METHOD

The easiest way to get a group to start doing the five-step method is to have a facilitator talk them through the steps; otherwise, I promise you, you will get scenic initiations that just literally manifest the input word. Really, without a process, an improviser's knee-jerk reaction is usually to literalize the input word.

So, get familiar with the steps, and then talk your group through them. Make sure they take the time and space necessary to have an open-ended, nonjudgmental cascade. Here is a transcript of me talking a group through the five-step method:

> "Everyone sit down and close your eyes. Really, close them. I know it's weird; close them anyway.
>
> First, I am going to give you a word. That is step 1, me giving you an input word. Your input word is 'midnight.'
>
> Now, step 2 is you having an open-ended cascade of thoughts, emotions, sensations, and memories based on the input word.
>
> What does that word make you think of? Make you feel? What does it make you remember? Make you see,

hear, or taste?

Just let these images, thoughts and feelings flow, even if they have nothing to do with the input word. Don't judge your cascade—just go with it."

At this point, I get everyone to stop and open his/her eyes. I know we have only done two steps, but I like to take a minute to ask the group what they experienced in their cascade. Everyone is usually pretty impressed with the variety of images, feelings, and memories that the group experienced during their cascade. Now back to the transcript:

"Okay, close your eyes again and let's do steps 1, 2, and 3. Your input word is 'star.'

What does that word make you think of? Make you feel? What does it make you remember? Make you see, hear, or taste?

Don't shortchange your cascade; allow yourself time and space to associate.

It's time for step 3: selection. Just select one thing from your cascade. Just pick anything that seems interesting to you. There is no right or wrong thing to pick; just pick one thing.

Now that you have selected your one thing from your cascade, it is time for step 4: specification. Take the thing you picked and focus on one specific aspect of it. If you selected a car, you can't manifest a whole car in a scene, but you can manifest the steering wheel, the trunk, or the backseat. So, focus the thing you selected down to one specific detail."

At this point, I have everyone open their eyes again and tell me what they selected and how they made it more specific. Because the improvisers are given the time and space to allow their imagination to work, usually everyone has a wildly specific and personal thing to share with the group. And this wildly specific and personal response to the input word feels a whole lot better than the panic of the void that most improvisers start scenes with.

So, everyone has gone through steps 1 to 4. They have taken an input word and processed it into a specific and personal response. I then ask the players to get on stage, one at a time, and manifest their specific personal response. They can do anything to manifest their response—all I ask is that they use their body and make their offer physical.

FIVE-STEP METHOD MANIFESTATION DRILL

Do this exercise after you talk through the five-step method a couple of times and the group seems to understand how to do it.

Have everyone line up on a back line. The back line gets a word and goes through the five-step method. One at a time, players step off the back line, making an initial physical offer by manifesting what they selected from their cascade. Have everyone do an initial physical offer inspired by the same word. You will see as many different responses to the input word as there are players.

This is a nonverbal exercise. Repeat the exercise until all the players can use the five-step method to do an initial physical offer automatically.

Side Coaching:
"Don't rush your cascade."
"How can you physicalize the thing you selected?"

MANIFESTATION DRILL WITH THE JOIN

Everyone stands on a back line. The back line gets a word and goes through the five-step method. A player steps off the back line and creates a initial physical offer by manifesting what he/she selected from his/her cascade, then the player who is making the initial physical offer is joined by another player. Make sure the players are already familiar with how to do the Join (See chapter 4).

Side Coaching:
"Look at what he is doing to start the scene—who can step out and join him?"
"You don't have to know what she is doing to join her. Join without knowing what she is doing."

THE FIVE-STEP METHOD WITH THE JOIN TO START SCENES

A player uses the five-step method to create an initial physical offer, and then another player joins that offer. After the Join is complete, the players begin a scene.

Some Tips

Make sure the players wait to speak until after the Join is complete.

Make sure the joiner gives the beginner the chance to speak first.

If the beginner does not have a verbal offer (and that is fine), then the joiner speaks first. This does not happen all that often.

The Join is not an entrance, so if the first line of the scene is a greeting like "Hi, Tom," then restart.

If the joiner joins by stopping the beginner from doing what they are doing, then they are not joining—they are cancelling.

The beginner does not own the scene; they are starting with something specific, but no one knows where it will go. There is no plan, and no one is in control.

Give and take.

Respond to the last thing said.

Yes and each other.

Side Coaching:
"Wait for the Join before you start; you will feel it when it happens."
"Do something physically with your body to join your partner."
"Think *we* instead of me."

Chapter 15
Step 4
Building the Agreement: The Noodles

So, you are using the five-step method to make an initial physical offer, and that offer is being joined by your partner (or vice versa). That's what I call starting scenes with joins, and for me every scene starts with a join.

If you consistently start scenes with joins, you will see how much can be established before you even speak. That is why we do joins at the top of scenes—to define scenic elements spontaneously and immediately—but a join doesn't do all the work. There is more work to be done at the top of a scene, after a join, to establish all five of the scenic elements. The agreement is not fully built until everyone knows what they are make-believing, and establishing all five of the scenic elements helps you do that. So, after you do a join, assess what you've built, and then add what has not been defined.

That's what I do at the top of a scene after every offer is made—I figure out what has been built, agree to it, and then make an offer that adds what has not yet been defined. I do that until all five scenic elements have been established and everyone in the scene knows what they are make-believing. This is what I call stage one of a scene: building the agreement or the noodles.

How do you get better at doing this?

I think there are two skills that are important to learn in order to be a good agreement builder. Here they are:

Skill 1: Start with the noodles

You need to know how to initiate scenes with scenic elements in mind. You need to be able to think, "I am going to initiate by establishing point of attack," or "I am going to initiate by establishing character." I do this during the manifestation step of the five-step method. When I step out to manifest the thing I selected from my cascade, I decide which element I want to establish with my initial physical offer. That way, I know at least one scenic element has been established.

Skill 2: Recognize the noodles

You need to know how to recognize the scenic elements created by your partner. You need to be able to think, "He just established point of attack," or "She just established character." I do this by being other-focused when my partner is making offers. While I am other-focused, I assess what scenic elements my partner created. That way, I know what I am agreeing to—the scenic element(s) my partner just established.

Exercises

Here are some exercises that will help you learn two important skills: starting scenes by establishing scenic elements and recognizing the scenic elements created by your partner.

RERUN

Have everyone stand on a back line. As always, use the five-step method with the Join to start scenes. After the Join, the beginner makes a verbal offer—he says his first line.

Then, before the joiner responds, the beginner repeats his first line.

At this point, pause the scene. With the scene paused, ask the joiner what scenic elements have been established by the beginner's first line of dialogue. Then restart the scene from the top and give the joiner a chance to respond to the first line of dialogue.

This exercise slows down the top of the scene so the joiner has time to fully understand what they are being given by their partner. Lots of times, the joiner does not even hear the first verbal offer of the scene because they are so self-focused. This exercise forces the joiner to be other-focused while the beginner is making the first verbal offer. This exercise teaches the second skill listed above: recognize the noodles.

Scenic Element Isolations: Round One

This exercise will train you to initiate scenes with scenic elements in mind; in other words, it will train you to start with the noodles.

As always, use the five-step method with the Join to start scenes, but before you start, select one scenic element that must be defined by the first player to speak.

Here is how it works:

Step 1: Select one element that must be defined with the first line of dialogue. Choose from character, relationship, environment, point of view, and point of attack.

Step 2: Get an input word, and go through the five-step method.

Step 3: One player (the beginner) steps out and makes an initial physical offer with the predetermined scenic element in mind.

Step 4: The beginner is joined by another player (the joiner).

Step 5: The beginner establishes the predetermined scenic element with his/her first line.

This exercise will help you guide the "cascade–select–specify–manifestation" process toward one of the five scenic elements. It will train you to think in scenic elements.

Repeat this exercise until you have had a chance to initiate with all five scenic elements in mind.

Some Tips

Every scene starts with a join.

Make sure the Join is complete before any player speaks.

Pick the scenic element you want to work on before you give the input word.

Everyone should have a very strong handle on what the scenic elements are. Make everyone give examples of each element so they can be confident when it comes time for them to initiate scenes. If a player does not understand point of attack, they are going to have a hard time defining that element with their first line of dialogue.

Make sure that your cascade includes thoughts, emotions, and memories. Just because this exercise asks you to manifest a specific scenic element with your first line, it doesn't mean you should limit your cascade. Keep the cascade wide open, and work toward manifesting whatever scenic element you picked before the scene.

Keep these scenes short (just a few lines), and talk after each one about how effective the first line was in defining the scenic element that you were isolating.

Scenic Element Isolations: Round Two

This round is similar to the first one, but now you give both players in the scene an element to define with their first line of dialogue. As always, use the five-step method with the Join to begin scenes. Also, decide who will be the beginner and who will be the joiner prior to the start.

Here are three of my favorite combinations for two-person scenes:

Beginner names the environment while pantomiming something in the space.

Joiner agrees to environment and adds point of attack.

Beginner names the environment while pantomiming something in the space.

Joiner establishes their character's point of view about the environment.

Beginner establishes joiner's character.

Joiner agrees to the character they were given and establishes beginner's character.

Make sure you train yourself to initiate with scenic elements as well as join with scenic elements so you have the ability to do both. They are different skills, and it is natural that you will be better at one than the other, but you want to be able to play both positions at the top of a scene.

Three-line Scenes: *Who, What, Where*

Again, have everyone form a back line. Use the five-step method with the Join to start two-person scenes. The scene only lasts three lines, and the players must use those three lines to define who the characters are, where the scene is taking place, and what the characters are doing there.

After three lines, the scene is over and a different pair does a new three-line scene.

This is a good exercise to get players used to providing the *who, what, where* at the top of the scene. Do enough three-line scenes, and providing the *who, what, where* will become automatic.

Note: Strictly speaking, "what you are doing" is not a scenic element, but your activity is one of the best ways to establish the *where*, or environment.

Side Coaching:
"Try to make the dialogue sound like real people talking."

Scene Setups

One of the best ways to show improvisers how great their work can be is to get them to be in a scene with the dramatic situation given to them. This just means that you define the five scenic elements for the improvisers before they start the scene. You don't tell them what will happen in the scene, but you give them the characters, relationship, environment, point of view, and point of attack. Then they get to play that scene.

Nothing convinces an improviser that the five scenic elements should be defined more than the success of a scene where it is defined for them. Think about it—all the hard work of building the agreement is done, and the improvisers get to just drop in to the world of the scene. When these scenes succeed, it's proof that if the elements are defined, the scene can be great.

These scenes are often truly awesome, and they give the improvisers a chance to be actors. You can use the success of these scenes as motivation for players to define the scenic elements for themselves in the future.

Try scene set-ups where you only define four elements, only define three elements, two elements, one element.

Side Coaching:
"Start with a join."
"Play with what you have been given."
"Relax and take your time, we have done all the hard work for you."

Chapter 16
Step 5
Finding Your Character's *How*: The Head, Heart, Body Method

Okay, so the goal is to make establishing the five scenic elements automatic every time you do a scene. That is what the exercises in chapter 15 were geared toward. Starting scenes with joins and creating a conscious process of defining scenic elements at the top of a scene is what I call *building the agreement*.

But honestly, there is one scenic element that is literally impossible to not start defining at the top of a scene: character. By the time you finish your first line of dialogue, you will have gone a long way in defining who you are in the scene.

Take a look at my definition of character from earlier in the book:

> **Character is created by what you do and how you do it, in the context of the world of the scene.**

Even before your character says his first line, you will have started to define your character's *how*. You character's *how* is the way they do stuff, and since you are starting scenes with joins, you will be doing stuff before you even speak. Starting scenes with joins means you also begin scenes with your character's *how*. So, the process of finding your character's *how* starts at the top of a scene and is fundamental to figuring out who your character is.

But what the heck is a character's *how*, anyway?

Here is what I mean when I use the word *how* in this context:

How does your character move? Are they fast or slow? Is your character clumsy or graceful? Do they stomp around the room or tread lightly?

Maybe your character does not move all that much.

How does your character stand? Do they stand up straight or slump over? Where do they hold their tension in their body?

How does your character sit? Are they relaxed and leaning back in their chair or tense and curled up into a tight ball? Are they somewhere in between?

How does your character make eye contact? Do they look people directly in the eye? Do they refuse to make eye contact?

How does your character talk? Do they love the sound of their own voice? Are they a character of few words? Do they speak in a dialect? Are they a fast talker or a quiet talker?

How does your character feel emotionally? Are they a happy

person? Are they stressed out? Are they trying to hide how they feel? Are they open with their emotions?

As you can see from all these questions, your character's *how* is the way they do stuff.

We experience your character's *how* by what they do and the way they do it. We see your character's behavior, their activity, their movement (or lack thereof), the way they carry themself, the way they talk, and that is how we know who your character is—by the way they do stuff.

But how do you do it? How do you figure out the way your character does what they do?

I think there are three ways into your character's *how*—your head, your heart, and your body. I call these three ways into your character's *how* the Head, Heart, Body method.

The Head, Heart, Body Method

Head (or thinking your way into *how*)

Think of a character. It could be a person you know, a character from literature, or even a classic stereotype like a spy or sorority girl or cowboy. Get a picture of that character in your brain, and then transform your body and voice into what you think that character's *how* would be like.

The character's *how* starts in your head with an idea, and then you alter your body and voice into that idea.

You don't even need to think of a whole character. You could just think of one specific idea about your character, like their age, gender, or what they do for a living, and then transform yourself into that *how*. The origination of the *how* starts in the brain. Your mind tells your body how to move, and your heart how to feel, and you transform into your character.

In my experience, this is the most common way improvisers create the *how*—by thinking of something specific and then doing it—but you can find your way into *how* without thinking.

Heart (or feeling your way into *how*)

At the top of a scene—before, during, or after a join—drop into an emotion, any emotion. Just drop into an emotion and really feel it. At this point, you won't even know why you feel your emotion, but that's not important right now; you will figure that out later. All that matters now is that you really drop into the emotion and allow the feeling to transform your body.

Keep doing whatever it is you're doing during the join, and keep feeling the emotion you dropped into—you will start to feel a transformation in your body. This emotional exploration will start to have a domino effect on how your body feels. It will also have a domino effect on your thinking.

That is how this *how* stuff works—you make one choice with your head, heart, or body, and it has a domino effect on your whole being. One small choice leads to a million other specific choices and discoveries. Your emotional state tells your body how to move while your body tells your head who you are, so you spontaneously discover your *how* through the domino effect.

You get to the same destination. You know who you are—you are a spy or a sorority girl or a cowboy. You just didn't preselect your character with your mind; you discovered your character by making a choice with your heart (the emotion you dropped into) and allowed the domino effect to help you fill in the rest of the blanks.

The domino effect is not restricted to discovering a character's *how*. I use it every time I improvise. You can find out more about the domino effect in the micro-technique chapter that begins on page 223.

Body (or doing your way into *how*)

While you are starting a scene with a join, change one thing about your body. You can change anything—where you hold your tension, how fast you move, your posture, a gesture—really, anything. Just make sure the change is different from your own body. If you have a straight posture, then give your character a slump; or if you keep your hands in your pockets, make your character use big gestures when they talk. This thing you are doing is the beginning of your transformation into the character's *how*.

This body change needs to be something you are doing through movement, gesture, posture, or held tension. Make sure you can actually feel the change in your body.

This body change will start to have a domino effect on the rest of your body. If you change one thing, you change everything. The change in your body's movement, gesture, posture, or held tension will also have a domino effect on your feelings and thoughts. Your body will tell your heart how to feel, and your heart will tell the head who you are.

You discovered your character by making a choice with your body, and then allowed the domino effect to help you fill in the rest of the blanks. The result is the same—you know who you are.

Exercises

The best exercise I know of to teach the Head, Heart, Body method is the Character Walk exercise, and it's a classic. Really, I have been doing Character Walk exercises since my first acting class. It is an oldie but a goody, and it works. This exercise will help you feel the transformation from your own personal *how* into your character's *how*.

Here are the basic steps to the Character Walk exercise:

> **Step 1**: Walk normally. Your regular old walk.
>
> **Step 2**: Get some kind of character input for inspiration (we'll talk about input below).
>
> **Step 3**: Allow the input to change something about the way you walk.
>
> **Step 4**: Explore how this character walks.
>
> **Step 5**: The exploration of the way this character walks leads to a series of choices and discoveries about who the character is (also known as the domino effect).

Let's address character input (from step 2 above). You can do the Character Walk exercise with any kind of input, just like you can inspire a scene with any kind of input. But I like to use the Character Walk exercise to isolate the type of input the players get to find their way into the character's *how*.

For example, if you do a series of Character Walk exercises using only occupations and stereotypes as inputs, then you will get better at thinking (Head) your way into *how*.

If you do a series of Character Walk exercises using only emotions as inputs, then you will get better at feeling (Heart) your way into *how*.

If you do a series of Character Walk exercises using only body/movement descriptions, like "walk with quick steps" or "hold your tension in your shoulders," as inputs, then you will get better at doing or moving (Body) your way into *how*.

So, let's get you better at using the Head, Heart, Body method to create a character's *how*.

CHARACTER WALK WITH HEAD (OR THINKING) INPUTS

Step 1: Walk normally. Your regular old walk.

It is important for the players to feel how they walk normally. This is their personal *how*. Ask them to feel where they hold tension or what part of their body they lead with. If the players are non-actors, give them a little time to get over their self-consciousness about this process. Nothing freaks a non-actor out more than walking around a space and being asked to "feel how they walk." Give these people a little extra time to normalize this new behavior.

Now everyone is walking around the space, and they have a handle on their own personal *how*—how they walk, how they make eye contact, where they hold tension. Time to move on to step 2.

Step 2: Get some kind of Head (or thinking-based) character input.

When you think your way into *how*, you have an idea of who the character is before you transform into the character's *how*. You think, "I'll be a cowboy," then start to walk and talk like a cowboy. The origination of the character was in the brain. So, to work this muscle, give the group inputs that are ideas for characters.

Start by giving the players stock character types as input, like spy, sorority girl, or cowboy. Something they can really see in their mind. The goal right now is not originality—it is to get the players to use what they see in their minds and put that in their bodies to find the character's *how*. We want to see big transformations from the player's personal *how* to the character's *how*, and stock characters help that happen.

After the players start to learn how to transform, then you can give them more open-ended, thinking-based inputs like age, gender, and occupation.

Step 3: Allow the input to change something about the way you walk.

The players take the character input they were given and come up with some idea of the character. Then they start to walk the way they think that character would walk. They consciously change their *how* into the character's *how*.

Step 4: Explore how this character walks.

You might have to encourage the players to change the way they walk more in order for them to really feel the transformation. You want the players to be able to really feel the difference between their walk and the character's walk. Sensing these differences will help you fill in the blanks. Encourage the players to hold off on making hard and fast decisions as to who this character is; ask them to just explore before they decide. By now, the character's walk is usually pretty different than the player's walk, and that's a good thing.

Step 5: The way this character walks leads to a series of choices and discoveries about who the character is (the domino effect).

As the players explore their characters' walks, the domino effect will start to take place. The specific way the character walks leads to a series of other choices and discoveries about who the character is.

You can facilitate the domino effect by asking the players rhetorical questions about their characters, like, "What is your name? How old are you? Are you married? What emotion are you feeling right now? Where do you hold your tension?"

Pretty soon, the players figure out that choices made in their minds have an effect on the heart and body, and, almost immediately, the domino effect takes place, and the *how* spreads to their whole being.

CHARACTER WALK WITH HEART (OR FEELING) INPUTS

Step 1: Walk normally. Your regular old walk.

It is important for the players to feel how they walk normally (see above).

Step 2: Get some kind of Heart (or feeling-based) character input.

When you feel your way into *how*, before you have any idea of who the character is, you drop into an emotion. The feeling is the origination of the character's *how*. So, to work this muscle, give the group inputs that are emotions.

Start by giving the players primary emotions such as joy, love, sadness, anger, fear, and surprise. Something they can really drop into. The goal is to get the players to put this feeling in their bodies to find the character's *how*. We want to see big transformations from the player's personal *how* to the character's *how*, and primary emotions help that happen.

After the players start to learn how to transform, then you can offer them subtler feeling-based inputs like affection, envy, or optimism.

Step 3: Allow the input to change something about the way you walk.

The players take the character input they were given, drop in, and really feel that emotion. Then they start to walk while feeling their emotion. The emotion will change how they walk.

Step 4: Explore how this character walks.

You might have to encourage the players to heighten the way they feel in order for them to really be aware of the transformation. You want the players to be able to really sense the difference between their walk and the character's walk. Feeling these differences will help you fill in the blanks. Encourage the players to hold off on making hard and fast decisions as to who this character is; ask them to just explore before they decide. By now, the character's walk is usually pretty different than the player's walk, and that's a good thing.

Step 5: The way this character walks leads to a series of choices and discoveries about who the character is (the domino effect).

As the players explore their characters' walks, the domino effect will start to take place. The specific way the character walks leads to a series of other choices and discoveries about who the character is.

You can facilitate the domino effect by asking the players rhetorical questions about their characters, like, "What emotion are you feeling right now? Did it change from the emotion you were given? What is your name? How old are you? Are you married? Where do you hold your tension?"

Pretty soon, the players figure out that choices made in their heart have an effect on the mind and body, and, almost immediately, the domino effect takes place, and the *how* spreads to their whole being.

CHARACTER WALK WITH BODY (OR DOING/MOVING) INPUTS

Step 1: Walk normally. Your regular old walk.

It is important for the players to feel how they walk normally (see above).

Step 2: Get some kind of Body or doing/moving-based character input.

When you move or do your way into *how*, before you have any idea of who the character is, you start doing stuff. You move first and think and feel later. This movement or act of doing is the origination of the character's *how*. So, to work this muscle, give the group some movement description as inputs.

Here's a list of some of the movement descriptors that I use so you can get a better idea about what I am talking about:

Quick walker • Slow walker • Heavy stepper • Light stepper
Head leads • Pelvis leads • Feet lead • Chest leads
Arms crossed • Hands in pockets • Jaw tension • Butt tension

So, you give the players an input that describes the way they move but dictates nothing else about the character. That way, the players can just explore by moving and doing. The goal is to get the players to move their bodies the way you described with the input. This suggested way of moving helps them find the character's *how*.

Step 3: Allow the input to change something about the way you walk.

The players walk with the input as inspiration. The movement description that was provided as input will change how they walk.

Step 4: Explore how this character walks.

You might have to repeat or elaborate the movement description in order for the players to really experience the transformation. You want the players to be aware of the difference between their walk and the character's walk. Sensing these differences will help you fill in the blanks. Encourage the players to hold off on making hard and fast decisions as to who this character is; ask them to just explore the movement before they decide. By now, the character's walk is usually pretty different than the player's walk, and that's a good thing.

Step 5: The way this character walks leads to a series of choices and discoveries about who the character is (the domino effect).

As the players explore their characters' walks, the domino effect will start to take place. The specific way the character walks leads to a series of other choices and discoveries about who the character is.

You can facilitate the domino effect by asking the players rhetorical questions about their characters like, "Why are your shoulders so tense? Why are you walking so fast; are you nervous about something? What emotion are you feeling right now? How old are you? What do you do for a living?"

Pretty soon, the players figure out that choices made in their body have an effect on the head and heart, and, almost immediately, the domino effect takes place, and the *how* spreads to their whole being.

Chapter 17
Step 6

Making Environment Specific, Real, and Automatic: The Where-four

As you can tell by now, my step-by-step method to create awesome scenes is a series of techniques I use to make building the agreement automatic.

I automatically do the five-step method to make my initial physical offer.

I automatically join my partner if he/she initiates the scene.

I automatically assess what scenic elements my partner has

established and add what has not yet been defined.

I automatically explore my character's *how* at the top of the scene by using the Head, Heart, Body method.

And in step 6, we are going to talk about making the environment automatic by using something I call the *Where-four*.

In my experience, most players think simply labeling their environment is all they need to do to establish it. They think, "I'll just say where I am, like a grocery store or a bank, and my job is done." They give the environment a label and then just stand there and talk. These players don't believe in the label they created for the environment, and they don't fully transform the stage into the physical world of the scene.

Why?

Because these players didn't do anything to make the environment real for themselves. They did not buy into the physical world of the scene. You have to participate in your environment to make it real. You have to touch, see, taste, hear, and smell your world in order to transform the stage into a make-believe place. If you just say, "Wow, this is a big barn," you have only taken the first step in creating the environment.

So, I have created a little system that helps the improviser get more involved with the scene's environment: the Where-four. I use it to make the environment specific and real for my character. If you define the Where-four, you will transform the label of your environment into a real place.

The Where-four
(in no particular order)

Placement
Exactly where in space your body is placed in relation to the other stuff that is in the environment—like sitting behind the wheel of your car or standing next to the water cooler at work.

Object
Anything in the space that you can see, hear, smell, taste, or touch. This includes other humans, sound, animals, wind, temperature, food, furniture—anything that can be experienced by you. In the Where-four, object is more than just three-dimensional stuff.

Activity
Anything you do to interact with any of the objects in this environment. Anything you touch. Anything you hear. Anything you smell. Anything you taste. Anything you see.

Time
This one is a little harder to define and requires a lengthier description.

When you are in an environment changes the type of place it is. For example, during the day in Central Park in New York City, the sun is out, people are everywhere having picnics—it's a happy place. But if you change the time and are walking through Central Park at night, you are alone and it's dark—that would be a scary place. So, when you are in a certain environment directly affects that environment.

The Where-four (placement, object, activity, and time) are the same ways you are connected to your environment in the real world. You always have a specific placement in your larger environment. You are always surrounded by specific objects, interacting with those objects in a specific way, at a specific time.

Placement, object, activity, and time are just how we relate to environment in the real world, so I think it's helpful to define them in the world of the scene.

Use yourself as an example. Right now, as you read this book, you are in a Where-four. In your current environment, you have a defined placement, object, activity, and time. Let's take a look.

Placement is where you are, specifically. Like right now, you are not just in your house—you are downstairs, in the living room, sitting on the grey couch, right next to an open window. Actually, that is where I am right now—that is my placement. What is your placement right now? Where are you specifically in space in relation to your larger environment?

Object is the stuff, physically and sensually, that is there with you in this specific place. What objects do you have around you right now? This book, your cellphone, the grey couch you are sitting on, the cup of coffee on the table in front of you, your wife talking on the phone in the other room—wait, those are my objects in my Where-four. What are the objects in your Where-four? They are anything you can see, touch, taste, smell, or hear right now.

Activity is everything you are interacting with. At this moment, you are interacting with this book, but you are interacting with a lot more than just that. Activity is anything your body is actually touching, seeing, hearing, smelling, and tasting in this specific location. Your senses are being stimulated by everything around you, and all of that stimulation is part of your environment. What stimulation you choose to interact with is your activity. Right now, the stimulation you are choosing to interact with is this book. Good choice.

Time is when the scene is taking place, but this does not refer to just the hour on the clock. For example, reading this book at your place of employment during work time is a very different environment than reading this book at your place of employment during your lunch hour. When you carry out an activity changes the atmosphere of the environment.

Now, you could use any of the Where-four to help you realize your environment. There is no correct order for the Where-four; you just start by defining any one—placement, object, activity, or time—and then the domino effect kicks in and fills in the blanks. If you truly buy into one of the Where-four, the other parts of the environment will start to take shape. And when you fully flesh out your environment, then some of the other scenic elements (character, relationship, point of view, and point of attack) are automatically defined.

Exercises

Here are some exercises that use the Where-four (placement, object, activity, and time) to help you get more involved with the scene's environment. Experience with these exercises will help make the environments you create more specific and real for your character.

SCENE PAINTING: REAL PLACE

One of the most effective ways to get the players involved with the scene's environment is to use a real place from their real lives. This exercise does just that.

Scene painting in improv is when the players describe, in detail, what is in the environment of the scene before the scene starts. In this exercise, one player gets on stage and describes a real place from their real life, like their bedroom or the office they work in. The more detail the better, so this process will take a few minutes.

After the space has been described, the player who described it and another player do a join and start the scene. The player who described the space can play themselves as their character or someone else—whatever makes sense for the scene.

In this exercise, the description of the space creates the objects in the environment, and the Join at the top of the scene creates placement and activity. So, three of the Where-four are taken care of before anyone even speaks. Time (when the scene is taking place) could be described as part of the scene painting or discovered spontaneously during the scene.

This exercise usually creates some great scene work, because the fully described environment helps ground the players in a reality.

SCENE PAINTING: IMAGINED PLACE

This is the same exercise as above, but now the place is made up. You can have one or more players doing the scene painting because it's not anyone's personal real place. Have the players that make the description do the scene. This will keep players from making ridiculous places that other people have to justify.

Have the players describe only the environment, and stay away from describing characters. Verbally illustrate what is in the space—not who is in the space.

Have the players do a join in the described environment to start the scene.

WHERE-FOUR ISOLATIONS

This exercise will train you to initiate scenes with placement, object, activity, and time in mind.

As always, use the five-step method with the Join to start scenes, but before you start, select one of the Where-fours that must be defined by the player who makes the initial physical offer (the beginner). Here is how it works:

Step 1: Select one of the Where-fours that must be defined by the player who makes the initial physical offer. Choose from placement, object, activity, and time.

Step 2: Get an input word and go through the five-step method.

Step 3: One player (the beginner) steps out and establishes one Where-four (placement, object, activity, or time) with his/her initial physical offer.

Step 4: The joiner joins the beginner.

Step 5: The scene starts.

This exercise will illustrate to your group that when you establish one of the Where-fours, the rest of the environment quickly starts to take shape. One specific choice in placement, object, activity, or time at the top of a scene leads to a series of choices and discoveries—the domino effect.

And, if you truly believe in your environment, the other scenic elements will reveal themselves to you as well. If you see, touch, hear, taste, and smell your environment, you will spontaneously discover your character. If you know where you are, you often know who you are. Do Where-four isolations until everyone in your group learns how to physically initiate placement, object, activity, and time.

OBJECT, ACTIVITY, EMOTION

In this exercise, you start with object. You imagine any object that could be in the environment, and remember, object in this context means anything you can experience with the five senses. First, you imagine an object and make it real for yourself. Make sure you can imagine experiencing the object with your senses.

After you select your object and make it real, start interacting with the object—this is activity. If your object is a song playing on the radio, then start to dance; if it's a gun, then start to clean it; if it's a chair, then lounge on it—interact in some specific way with the object.

Now, during this interaction, add an emotion. It does not matter what emotion you drop into. Maybe the activity will inspire a feeling, or perhaps you will just decide to drop into the emotion of happiness. Either way is fine; just do the activity while you drop into the emotion.

Here are the steps again:

Step 1: Object—Imagine an object and make it real for yourself.

Step 2: Activity—Interact with the imagined object.

Step 3: Emotion—During the interaction, drop into an emotion.

Do these three steps, and you will spontaneously define the scenic elements of environment and character.

If you truly make the object real for yourself, and if, during your interaction with the object, you really drop into an emotion, then the reason you feel the emotion will become clear to you. You will know why you feel your emotion while you are doing your activity, and you will know who your character is. No kidding—it works like magic.

Why?

Because character is defined by what you do and how you do it in the context of the world of the scene.

It is the combination of the specific thing you are doing (your activity with your object) and how you are doing it (your emotion) that will spontaneously define who you are (your character).

As you can see, this exercise combines the Where-four approach to environment with the Head, Heart, Body method for finding a character's *how*. The scenic elements of environment and character are so closely linked that they actually overlap. They overlap in the use of activity because you can use activity to establish environment and character.

Think about it—when you do an activity, you automatically define object and placement, and that creates environment.

And when you do an activity, you will always have some kind of *how* going on in the way you do it. Activity creates *how*, and how you do what you do creates character.

So, environment and character are created simultaneously with activity.

After you master object, activity, and emotion, try plugging other things into step 1 and 3. In step 1, you can plug in placement, object, or time, and in step 3, you can try plugging in head or body. Step 2 is always activity.

So, here is another way to look at the 3 steps:

Step 1: Imagine placement, object, or time.
Note: Placement and time automatically create object.

Step 2: Activity—Interact with imagined object.

Step 3: How—During interaction, use the Head, Heart, Body method to find the character's *how*.

Do this exercise until everyone in your group can effectively combine the Where-four and the Head, Heart, Body method to create environment and character.

FOUR-PLAYER SCENE WITH WHERE-FOUR ASSIGNMENTS

This exercise needs a better name, but it plays just like it sounds. Get four players on stage, assign which player is going to establish what part of the Where-four at the top of the scene, give them a word, and let them go. One player establishes placement, one player establishes object, one player establishes activity, and one player establishes time.

This exercise will guarantee that the Where-four will be defined at the top of a scene.

Chapter 18
Step 7
Adding the Sauce: Relationship and Point of View

So, the first six steps are all about starting scenes with joins and establishing scenic elements. In steps 5 and 6, you learned that character and environment are practically automatic at the top of a scene, because when you start scenes with joins, you start scenes with activity by interacting with something in the world of the scene. When you interact with the objects in the scene, including your partner, you automatically create character and environment.

Why?

Because while doing your activity, you start to discover your character's *how*, and that will lead you to who you are.

And when you do any activity, you automatically create object and placement in the environment. Activity, object, and placement are all part of the Where-four. If you define the Where-four, you make your environment real.

Okay, so starting with activity is a pretty big deal in my methodology. Starting with activity gives you the *who*, *what*, *where* of the scene—who you are, where you are, and what you are doing. And that is a strong start to building the agreement.

But here in step 7, it's time to add the sauce (or how your character feels about what is going on in the scene). That's why we worked so hard to build the agreement in the first place—to play with our character's point of view.

So, step 7 is about your character's point of view, but not just any point of view. Step 7 focuses on your character's point of view about their scene partner. That's the point of view we are going to play with in step 7—the one our character has about the other character(s) in the scene.

As I said earlier in the book, your character will have lots of different points of view about all the different things in their world, but we are looking for the one point of view that gets more and more intense over time. And for me, the point of view that gets more and more intense over time is caused by my scene partner. Eventually, my scene partner does or says something that effects me, and that effect is the point of view that gets heightened. This point of view that gets heightened is the character's Primary Emotional Drive.

So, step 7 is the discovery and heightening of your character's Primary Emotional Drive, and I call my system of doing this the *process of relationship*.

Here is the step-by-step method for the process of relationship.

Step 1: Create connections between the characters by establishing the following Relationship Components: history, emotion, status, physicality, space, and sensuality.

Step 2: The Relationship Components create a cause-and-effect pattern of behavior between the characters.

Step 3: This cause and effect is repeated and heightened by the characters.

Step 4: The repetition and heightening of cause and effect forces the characters to intensify their Primary Emotional Drive.

In step 2 above, "a cause-and-effect pattern of behavior between the characters" just means that the characters have a strong and recognizable point of view about each other. And in step 3, when I say the "cause and effect is repeated and heightened by the characters," I just mean that the characters keep doing what they are doing to get a bigger and bigger response from their partner.

You might recognize the process of relationship (steps 1–4 above) because it is the same process as heightening point of view that I talk about in chapter 7. So, if you follow these steps, you kill two birds with one stone—you explore relationship and you heighten the scene.

The key to this entire process is establishing how the characters are connected—the Relationship Components. These six ways characters are connected—history, emotion, status, physicality, space, and sensuality—are what create cause and effect between the characters.

Below, you will find exercises that help you initiate scenes by establishing Relationship Componentry at the top of a scene.

Relationship Componentry Exercises: Disclaimer

Before we move into the Relationship Componentry exercises, I have a little disclaimer.

Relationship Components—history, emotion, status, physicality, space, and sensuality—are the six ways characters are connected and mirror the ways we are connected to people in our real lives. These exercises are a little risky because they skip establishing character and environment at the top of a scene and go straight to the relationship and cause and effect between the characters.

Because the players start scenes by establishing one of the six relationship components, these exercises often create tension and conflict between the characters, which is the cause and effect I keep talking about. So, it is important to note that the tension and conflict at the top of these scenes is not a function of the player's anxiety about doing improv. When you initiate with relationship components, you automatically create cause and effect between the characters, so tension and conflict are just part of the deal with these exercises.

I think you have to master the first six steps in my methodology before you can handle Relationship Componentry. So, make sure your group has a lot of experience with the first six steps before you do these exercises.

Other things to keep in mind when doing these exercises:

You can initiate positive relationship components as well as negative ones.

Play with extremes—give yourself permission to yell, scream, laugh, and cry.

In improv, there is no real violence and no real sex. We are going to take risks, but we are also going to create boundaries.

For these exercises, you do not have to start scenes with joins.

The goal of establishing relationship components is to create cause and effect between the players, and that just means characters will have a strong and recognizable point of view about each other. So, when a strong and recognizable point of view about each other happens, it should not be a surprise.

Characters are going to get their feelings hurt—they are going to say things that would be mean to say in real life, and that is okay.

Enough with the disclaimers; here come the exercises. The following exercises teach how to initiate scenes by establishing history, emotion, status, physicality, space, and sensuality.

Relationship Componentry Exercises: History

Before you do the following exercises, review the idea that our past with another person effects our present with that person. Get everyone in the group to imagine a person from their real life. They need to pick a person around whom they change their behavior. You know, an ex-lover, a high school coach they looked up to, a best friend—whoever; just make sure the shared history affects the player in the present.

Ask the players how their behavior would change if their real person were in the room right now.

What, specifically, would change because that person was in the room?

Would they become more shy or nervous? More confident or outgoing?

The specific way a player's "behavior would change if his/her real person was in the room right now" is the cause and effect that is created by their shared history.

The way you are in the present is created by your past.

Now that you and your group recognize that shared history effects how we relate to the people in our present, let's take a look at how we can play with that technique in scenes.

IMAGINED PAST: REAL PERSON

This exercise teaches you how to "play a history" to your partner. You will learn how to treat your scene partner as if they were a person in your real life. But remember, your partner's character is not the person from your real life. They are not playing your ex-lover, a high school coach you looked up to, or your best friend—they are playing a character you treat in the same way as your ex-lover, a high school coach you looked up to, or your best friend.

Here is the exercise:

Get two players on stage—player A and player B. Ask player A to think of a person from their real life that would affect their behavior in the present. After player A thinks of their person, give the pair a mundane activity to do during the scene. During the scene, both players do the activity. As they play the scene, player A behaves as if player B were the person from his/her real life, but player B is not assuming the role of the person from player A's real life.

Player B can be whomever they want but must do the activity.

This exercise creates a scene in which player A is playing a history to their partner. Remind player A that their scene partner's character is not the person from their real life. Player A might want to refer to shared experiences from their real past, so encourage them to stay in the present and focus on their *how*.

Here are some variations: try this exercise without giving the players a mundane activity; try it with a location as the input. Try it with just a word and the five-step method to start the scene.

IMAGINED PAST: MADE-UP PERSON

Do the same exercise, but now, instead of player A thinking of a person from their real life, they create a person with their imagination. Now player A is not limited by their personal experience—they can imagine anyone, as long as it affects the way they relate to their partner in the present.

Player B can be whomever they choose to be.

Give the pair a mundane activity to do during the scene, and remind player A to keep the dialogue in the present. Often, players want to discuss the past and why they are behaving as they are. What we want is the behavior in the present rather than the discussion of the past.

What you want the players to get out of these exercises is the ability to play a history to their partner. Our history with a person colors everything we do when we are around that person. It is a powerful tool to get the characters connected. As I stressed earlier, if you can imagine your past, you can play your present.

Have your group do these exercises until they know what it feels like to play a history.

Relationship Componentry Exercises: Emotion

Our emotional connection with our partner is the beating heart of a scene. Great scene work is fed by how the characters feel emotionally about each other.

Our emotional point of view about our partner is what gets heightened during the scene. Ultimately, how you feel about the other character(s) in the scene is the key to great scene work.

Here are some exercises that help you initiate an emotional connection with your partner at the top of a scene.

EMOTIONAL MANIPULATION: OTHER

Get two players on stage—player A and player B. Player A initiates a scene with a line of dialogue that manipulates player B's emotional state. Player A says something that causes player B to feel a specific emotion, something like "Janet, you look great in that dress," or "Thomas, you have been late three times this week. One more time, and you're fired." Player A needs to make it clear what emotion he/she is trying to cause in player B.

Player B receives the first line and allows him or herself to be manipulated into the emotion that player A is trying to create within them.

Starting the scene with an emotional manipulation creates a strong cause and effect right off the bat. Allow the scene to play out, and see what develops between the characters. Because this exercise starts with point of view, you will have to encourage the players to establish the other scenic elements after the first two lines of the scene; otherwise, the character point of view can overpower the scene.

You will find that player B often resists being manipulated by player A. If you see this happening, let the player know they are resisting their partner. Encourage player B to transform into the emotional state that player A is trying to cause within them. If player A is trying to make player B happy, then player B should allow herself to be manipulated into happiness. Allow yourself to be manipulated. This exercise teaches that skill.

You can set the scene in a location, give them an activity, or just give them a word as input and see what they come up with.

Sometimes, players feel self-conscious when they manipulate their partner into a negative emotion. Remind them that he/she is not saying those horrible things to his/her partner—the character is. Also, some players refuse to manipulate their partner into a positive emotion. You should be able to work in both directions. If a member of your group only manipulates other players in one direction (positive or negative), let them know. The goal is to be able to do both equally well.

Some players just can't stand the word *manipulate*. It does have a rather negative connotation. But I love the word in this context. I love being transformed by my partner's strong and clear offers. That is what I am trying to do when I improvise—transform into my character and transport into the world of the scene. A strong manipulation at the top of a scene just makes the transformation that much easier to accomplish. So, be proud of how strong and clear your manipulations can become, and work on being flexible when you partner tries to manipulate you.

EMOTIONAL MANIPULATION: SELF

In this exercise, player A manipulates their own emotions rather than those of their scene partner.

Get two players on stage—player A and player B. Player A initiates a scene with a line of dialogue that establishes their own emotional state as caused by their scene partner, player B. Player A starts the scene with a response to something player B said or did before the scene started. Player A's first line might be something like "Thanks Rob, you're right, I do look great in this dress," or "I'm sorry for being late again, Mr. Roberts; it won't happen again."

So, the first line of the scene is player A's response to something that happened before the scene started. During this first line, player A declares how they feel about what just happened.

The second line of the scene is player B's response to player A. Player B's response should make player A feel their emotion—more. If player A's first line is "Thanks Rob, you're right, I do look great in this dress," then player B's job is to make player A feel even more attractive. If player A's first line is "I'm sorry for being late again, Mr. Roberts; it won't happen again," then player B's job it to make player A feel even more sorry.

As you can see, this exercise skips building the agreement and goes directly to heightening. These scenes require the players to add the other scenic elements as they are heightening each other's emotional points of view.

A common problem with this exercise is when player A's first line establishes how they feel about the situation or a character that is not in the scene. For example, if they start a scene with "I can't believe it rained on my wedding day," that initiation establishes how the character feels about the circumstance, not their scene partner. This exercise requires that the first line establish a feeling caused by your scene partner. We want the cause and effect to be between the characters.

WARNING

Emotional manipulation exercises can get heightened very fast. Make sure to encourage your group to go for extremes, but create a safe space to explore. If the emotions get too intense for an individual, honor that person's boundaries. Take your time with emotional manipulations; the first time you try this exercise, just get acquainted with the process. You can go deeper as your group gets used to these exercises. I have found that these emotional exercises can bring a group closer together and increase trust and support.

Relationship Componentry Exercises:
Status

Status is the most difficult component to play with because it is the most misunderstood. If you ask a player to lower their partner's status, they will insult their partner and boss them around. If you ask a player to heighten their partner's status, they will compliment them and become a servant.

People think status is what they say. Sure, insults, commands, and compliments will create status, but how do you go beyond master/servant scenes?

Think of status as something you do rather than something you say.

Status has so much more to do with eye contact and how we move and speak than it does with the sentences coming out of our mouth. So, the first step in playing with status is exploring movement that creates status. Here is an exercise that will help you learn how to play your status rather than *say* your status.

STATUS WALK

This exercise uses the Character Walk exercise to discover movement that communicates high and low status, or what I call *status values*.

Step 1: Walk normally. Your regular old walk.

Step 2: Status input (more about this below).

Step 3: Allow the input to change something about the way you walk, move, and gesture.

Step 4: Explore how this character moves.

Step 5: The exploration of how this character moves leads to a series of movements and gestures that have a defined status value.

By now, your group is familiar with the Character Walk exercise. One great thing about this exercise is that you can use any kind of input in step 2 to create a character. In the status walk exercise, you use status inputs to physically explore character movement and discover ways of walking, gesturing, and moving that communicate high- or low-status values. You can use this exercise to discover characters that are easily recognizable as high or low status just by watching how they move.

Here is the theory: certain movements, like holding eye contact or touching your face, are status communicators. So, by using the status walk exercise, your group can discover these status communicators for themselves. You will be able to explore what held eye contact feels like, and you will come to know that it creates high status for the person doing the holding. The goal is to create a vocabulary of status communicators that your group can use to play status to their partner.

Remember, status is relative. If I play low status, that means I am low as compared to my partner. If I play high status, then I am high as compared to my partner. If you play status, you automatically connect to your partner because your status helps define their status.

Here is a list of status inputs I use during step 2 of the status walk exercise to get players to feel high and low status in their bodies with how they move.

Animal Inputs:

High status: lion, tiger, elephant, shark, rooster, eagle, cat

Low status: rat, hyena, squirrel, mouse, fly, deer, puppy, lizard

Character Types/Occupation Inputs:

High status: judge, movie star, Knight of the Round Table, corporate CEO, doctor, snooty French waiter, magician, cop

Low status: thief, ball boy, personal assistant, beggar, drug addict

Circumstances/Dramatic Situations

High status: winning an award, getting married, scolding a dog, giving a speech

Low status: Nervous job interviewee, knocking on a door when you are late, asking for a favor, confronting your boss

These are just suggested inputs to get the players to transform their bodies. I am not saying a lion is always high status, as it is completely possible to play a low-status lion, but I have found that these inputs work to get the players to feel status in their bodies.

These inputs only exist to get the players to explore, with their bodies, how they might move with this input in mind. As they explore, they will discover movements and gestures that have defined status values. If an input that is on my high-status list creates low status for your group, go with that—whatever works to get you and your group to play status with your bodies.

As you give the players these inputs, you will see the quality of their movement change. The animal input *lion* will get players to puff out their chests as they glide confidently around the space. The animal input *squirrel* will get the players to touch their faces with their hands and scamper randomly around the stage. They won't be thinking, "I want to play high or low status," they will just be moving with the animal as inspiration. The benefit of this exercise is that it helps the players feel high and low status in their bodies. After a player learns how it feels in the body to play high or low status, they can create a personal list of specific movements that communicate their character's status.

Below is my list of specific movements that have status values for me. These are the kinds of movements and gestures you are trying to discover with the status walk exercise. As you do the status walk exercise, create your own list of movements and gestures that you think communicate status values.

My incomplete list of movements and gestures that create status:

HIGH	LOW
held eye contact	minimal eye contact
head remains still when talking	eye contact held for short time
slower movements	quick movements
consistent pace	hand touching face
low voice	high-pitched voice
relaxed posture	physical tension
slight smile	laughter
open chest	hands in pockets
keeping focus at eye level	looking up or down
feet planted in one spot	shifting weight back and forth
feet parallel	feet pointed in
tempo of movement remains consistent	tempo of movement changes often

In my experience, if you do stuff from the high-status column, then your character's status will go up, and if you do stuff from the low-status column, then your character's status will go down.

What I think is awesome about creating your own personal list of movements and gestures that create status is that they work in any situation. You can do any of these status value movements in any dramatic situation while you are playing any character because these status communicators do not dictate anything about the content of the scene.

It does not matter what the scenic agreement is—you can always add a movement or gesture for your character that creates high or low status.

Why can you, no matter what the scenic agreement, always add a status value movement or gesture for your character?

Because there is no such thing as an appropriate status for your character or situation. Even if your partner makes you the president of the United States with his/her first offer, you can still add the low-status movement of minimal eye contact to your character, because there is no appropriate status for president of the United States.

So, practice the status walk exercise until your body knows how to do high- and low-status movements and gestures. Make your own personal list of status value movements and gestures, and be sure to try the actions on my list. After you master the ability to play status with movement and gesture, you can move on to the next few exercises.

STATUS REPEAT

Get two players up—player A and player B—and have them do a short scene.

Give them an activity as input, and have them do the activity during the scene. The scene needs to be short because the players are going to repeat it. After the players do their short scene, give each player a status value to play while they are repeating the scene. For example, give player A high status and player B low status for the repeat. Then have the players repeat the scene with their new status values in mind.

If the players are anxious about remembering what they did during the scene, allow them to review the scene before they repeat it.

When the players repeat the scene, they do all the same lines and movements they did the first time, but now they add stuff from their personal list of status communicators. Because the dialogue and blocking for the scene is set, the players can't use what they say to manifest their status value during the repeat. This teaches the players to manifest status with what they do instead of what they say. You want to be able to play status with your whole body.

You can assign any status combination to the players when they repeat the scene: A high, B low; A low, B high; A high, B high; or A low, B low. Each status combination creates a different dynamic, and status repeat is a great exercise to introduce the next concept in status play: status transactions.

A status transaction is when a character does or says something to change his/her own or another character's status. You might have already found in the status repeat exercise that when a player plays low status, he/she inadvertently raises their scene partner's status. The lowering of one character's status creates the heightening of the other character's status. These changes in relative status between the characters are called *status transactions* and are powerful tools in comedy.

I have stressed many times that improv is acting, and that comedy is a by-product of the cooperation between the players, but I am not blind to the fact that most improv is comedic. I am not anti-comedy; I just don't think setting out to be funny is an effective way to achieve your goal.

But if you want to create comedy, there is one surefire way to do it—the status transactions. If you want to make an audience laugh, lower someone's status—anyone's; it doesn't matter. If you lower your own status, the audience laughs. If you lower your scene partner's status, the audience laughs. You can even lower the audience's status, and they will laugh. Status transactions automatically yield laughter. If you don't believe me, try these status transaction exercises and see what happens.

STATUS TRANSACTION EXERCISES
LOWER SELF: ROUND ONE

Get two players on stage—player A and player B. Have player A lower their own status during the course of the scene. They do not have to start as a low-status character, but they must lower their own status throughout the scene. Player B can play the scene any way they want.

LOWER SELF: ROUND TWO

Get two players on stage—player A and player B. Have both players lower their own statuses during the course of the scene. They do not have to start as low-status characters, but they must lower their own statuses throughout the scene.

Remember, the primary way you lower your status is with your personal list of status communicators; these are the low-status movements and gestures that you discovered while doing the status walk exercise. You can use those movements and gestures with any character in any situation, so make sure you use them to lower your own status in these scenes.

Sometimes you have to be a little more aggressive to really lower your status. So, here is another list of status-lowering behaviors:

Fail at doing something.
Get something wrong.
Insult yourself.
Submit to the will of others.
Reveal a fault.
Ask for help.
Admit a lack of knowledge or skill.
Break something valuable.
Laugh.
Cry.
Lose control of your emotions.
If nothing else works, become a servant.

Here's a special note about status transactions:
You will find that there are two ways to lower the status of your character. You can lower your own status, or you can heighten your partner's status. If you heighten your partner's status without equally heightening your own, you effectively lower your own status.

This is true with all status transactions. If you heighten your partner's status without heightening your own, then your status is going to go down. If you lower your partner's status without lowering your own, then your status is going to go up, because status is relative.

In the *lower self* exercises, we are isolating a type of status transaction so the players can learn the technique of lowering their own statuses. For the sake of the *lower self* exercises, make sure the players are not only heightening their scene partner in order to lower themselves.

LOWER OTHER: ROUND ONE

Get two players on stage—player A and player B. Have player A lower player B's status during the course of the scene. Player A can play any status they want, but they must lower player B's status throughout the scene.

Player B does not have to start the scene in low status, but they must allow their status to be lowered by player A.

LOWER OTHER: ROUND TWO

Get two players on stage—player A and player B. Player A lowers player B's status during the course of the scene, and player B lowers player A's status during the course of the scene. The players do not have to start as low-status characters, but they must lower each other's statuses throughout the scene.

Remember, both players must allow their status to be lowered by their scene partner. As you allow your status to be lowered, you start to use status-communicating movement and gesture to show your lower status. Lots of players resist having their status lowered—it is as if they think their personal status is being lowered. If you see this resistance, point it out to the player. Allowing your own status to be lowered by another player is fundamental for an improviser. It is natural to defend your status, but just because you do, it doesn't mean you are successful at keeping it. The character can defend their high status, but the improviser needs to realize that status is meant to be lowered.

Sometimes you have to be a little aggressive to lower your partner's status, so here is list of ways to lower your partner's status:

>Do something to them that forces them to do low-status movement and gesture.
>Make your partner touch their face.
>Make your partner laugh.
>Make your partner break eye contact.
>Have them fail at doing something.
>Make them lose at something.
>Insult them.
>Make them submit to your will or the will of others.
>Reveal their fault.
>Offer them help.
>Admit a mutual lack of knowledge or skill.
>Get them to break something valuable.
>Laugh at them.
>Make them cry.
>Make them lose control of their emotions.
>Get them to match your low-status movement and gesture.
>If nothing else works, make them a servant.

In the *lower other* exercises, we are isolating a type of status transaction so the players can learn the technique of lowering their partner's status. For the sake of the *lower other* exercises, make sure the players are not only heightening themselves in order to lower their scene partner.

HEIGHTEN SELF: ROUND ONE

Get two players on stage—player A and player B. Have player A heighten their own status during the course of the scene. They don't have to start as a high-status character, but they must heighten their own status throughout the scene. Player B can play the scene any way they want.

HEIGHTEN SELF: ROUND TWO

Get two players on stage—player A and player B. Have both players heighten their own status during the course of the scene. They do not have to start as high-status characters, but they must heighten their own status throughout the scene.

Remember, the primary way you heighten your status is with your personal list of status communicators; these are the movements and gestures with a high status that you discovered while doing the status walk exercise. You can use those movements and gestures with any character in any situation, so make sure you use them to heighten your own status in these scenes.

Sometimes you have to be a little more aggressive to really heighten your status. So, here is another list of status-heightening behaviors.

Succeed at doing something.
Get something right.
Compliment yourself.
Make others submit to your will.
Reveal an asset.
Offer help.
Show off your knowledge or skill.
Fix something valuable.
Smile just a little.
Comfort someone.
Control your emotions.
If nothing else works, become a king or queen.

In the *heighten self* exercises, we are isolating a type of status transaction so the players can learn the technique of heightening their own status. For the sake of the *heighten self* exercises, make sure the players are not *lowering other* to *heighten self*.

HEIGHTEN OTHER: ROUND ONE

Get two players on stage—player A and player B. Have player A heighten player B's status during the course of the scene. Player A can play any status they want, but they must heighten player B's status throughout the scene.

Player B does not have to start the scene in high status, but they must allow their status to be heightened by player A.

HEIGHTEN OTHER: ROUND TWO

Get two players on stage—player A and player B. Player A heightens player B's status during the course of the scene, and player B heightens player A's status during the course of the scene. The players do not have to start as high-status characters, but they must heighten each other's statuses throughout the scene.

Remember, both players must allow their status to be heightened by their scene partner. As you allow your status to be heightened, you start to use status-communicating movement and gesture to show your higher status.

Sometimes you have to be a little aggressive to heighten your partner's status, so here is a list to help you do it:

Do something to them that forces them to do high-status movement and gesture.
Get your partner to relax.
Get your partner to move slowly.
Get your partner to hold eye contact.
Get them to succeed at doing something.
Make them win at something.
Compliment them.
Make them stand up to the will of others.
Reveal their skill and beauty.
Accept their help.
Admit a mutual abundance of knowledge or skill.
Ask them to fix something valuable.
Help them control their emotions.
Get them to match your high-status movement and gesture.
If nothing else works, make them a king or queen.

In the *heighten other* exercises, we are isolating a type of status transaction so the players can learn the technique of heightening their partner's status. For the sake of these *heighten other* exercises, make sure the players are not *lowering self* to *heighten other*.

Here are a couple of other things to think of when learning how to play with status.

You will find that as an improviser, you have a natural or default status position. This is normal, but you don't want to be trapped into your default status. You want to be able to transform into any status at any time, and that is what the above exercises will help you do.

As you play with status, you will discover that you are better at playing a certain type of status. You might find that you love playing low status or that you are really good at playing high status. This is what I call your *status specialty*, and it is natural that you would be better at one type of status destination. No need to fight what works—if you are good at having your status lowered, then go for it. Just make sure you can go the other way if the scene needs you to play a high-status character.

MINIMUM AND MAXIMUM STATUS TRANSACTIONS

When players first start playing with status, they usually use *maximum status transaction*, which means that when they lower or heighten status, they lower or heighten it completely. However, with experience, you can learn to use a lighter touch when you change your own or your partner's status. These smaller changes in a character's status are called *minimum status transactions*, and they mirror the way status works in the real world. If you want to master using status in improv scenes, you must learn to use minimum status transactions, maximum status transactions, and everything in between.

Relationship Componentry Exercises: Physicality, Sensuality, and Space

I look at physicality, sensuality, and space as one big messy component dealing with the player's bodies, what they are sensing, and where they are in space. Whenever you establish any one of these three components, you automatically establish the other two, so I bundle physicality, sensuality, and space together.

Here are some things to think about when dealing with physicality, sensuality, and space.

Consider that physicality is your body, your scene partner's body, and how they are connected. Are they in contact? What does that contact say about the characters? Are they out of contact? What does their lack of contact say about the characters?

Sensuality is what your character and your scene partner's character are experiencing with the five senses. What sensual experience are you causing in your partner? What sensual experiences are they causing in you? Pain? Pleasure? What do these sensual experiences say about how the characters are connected?

The spatial relationship among the characters is what I call *space*. The player's bodies in space create a picture, but what does that picture mean? How much space is between the characters? Where are the characters focused? Are they moving toward or away from each other? Are they sitting, standing, or lying on the ground? Bodies in space create a picture—what do these pictures say about how the characters are connected?

Below are some exercises that help you initiate scenes using physicality, sensuality, and space. Remember, when you establish one of these components, the other two come along for the ride.

PHYSICALITY EXERCISES

SLOW-MOTION SWORD FIGHT

Get two players on stage, and have them pantomime a sword fight in slow motion. This exercise is a great way to get the players to see just how connected the characters are through physicality. During the slow-motion sword fight, there will be contact and distance and attacking and defending, and at every point in time, the players will know how they are connected. The characters will physically relate to each other moment by moment. Every action taken by one character will create a physical reaction in the other—the characters will be living in a cause-and-effect relationship.

The physical act of sword fighting will tell the players who they are to each other.

HEADLOCK: STARTING SCENES IN A POSE THAT DEFINES THE RELATIONSHIP

This is another exercise to help players create the kind of physicality at the top of a scene that defines who the characters are to each other.

I call this exercise *Headlock*, because I will often put a student in a headlock to demonstrate how it works. I put a student in a headlock and ask the rest of the players how much you know about the relationship between the players just by seeing one guy put another guy in a headlock. Then I ask the players to imagine that this headlock is a metaphor for these two characters' entire relationship. If this headlock is a metaphor for how these characters relate to each other, it becomes a heck of lot more important.

I would argue that starting scenes with joins gives the players an opportunity to discover a physical metaphor for how these characters relate every single time they improvise, and that is exactly what this exercise does. This exercise requires that you create a two-person pose at the top of the scene that defines your relationship with your partner.

Here's how to do the exercise:

Get two players on stage. You can give them some kind of input or not; it doesn't matter. Ask the players to get into a pose that defines the relationship between the two characters.

A player can think of the pose ahead of time or spontaneously discover one. If they think of a pose ahead of time, like a headlock, they might have to ask their partner to do something in order to make the pose make sense. For example, I could ask my partner to put his/her arms up and then I could aim a gun at them to define our relationship as robber and victim.

If you want to create the pose spontaneously, you are just going to be doing a join with your partner. Just remember in this exercise, you have to create a pose that tells us who these characters are to each other.

I think it is very helpful to talk to your group about the types of physical poses that communicate relationship while you do this exercise. You might even want to create a list of classic physical poses that communicate relationship—like hug, kiss, shoot-out, and headlock, just to name a few. If your group is having difficulty creating poses that define relationship, have them practice the ones on your list. That way, they can see the type of physicality that creates relationship and use it as inspiration.

The goal of this exercise is to help you learn how to create, with your partner, the type of physicality that defines who the characters are to each other at the top of a scene.

SENSUALITY EXERCISES

SENSUAL MANIPULATION: OTHER

This exercise is similar to the emotional manipulation exercises found earlier in the chapter, starting on page 175.

Get two players on stage—player A and player B. Player A initiates a scene by causing a sensual experience in player B. Player A does something that causes player B to have a specific sensual experience, something like tickling player B or breathing in player B's face. Player A needs to make it clear what sense he/she is trying to stimulate in player B.

Player B receives the stimulus and allows himself/herself to be manipulated into the sensation that player A is trying to create in them.

Starting the scene with a sensation creates a strong cause and effect right off the bat. Allow the scene to play out, and see what develops between the characters.

You will find that player B often resists being manipulated by player A. If you see this happening, let the player know they are resisting their partner. Encourage player B to be transformed by the sensation that player A is trying to give them. If player A is trying to tickle player B, then player B should allow himself/herself to be tickled.

You can set the scene in a location or just give them a word as input and see what they come up with.

SENSUAL MANIPULATION: SELF

In this exercise, player A manipulates their own senses rather than those of his/her scene partner.

Get two players on stage—player A and player B. Player A initiates a scene by experiencing a sensation caused by their scene partner, player B. Player A starts the scene with a response to something player B did before the scene started. Player A's first line might be something like, "Ouch, Rob, you hit me right in the face," or "Janet, you smell great, is that a new perfume?"

So, the first line of the scene is player A's response to something that happened before the scene started. During this first line, player A declares what sensual experience they are having.

A common problem with this exercise is when player A's first line establishes a sensation caused by the environment or a character that is not in the scene. For example, if they start a scene with the line, "Wow, it's cold out here," that initiation establishes a sensation caused by the environment, not their scene partner. This exercise requires that the first line establish a sensation caused by your scene partner. We want the cause and effect to be between the characters.

SPACE EXERCISES

STAGE PICTURE: ROUND ONE

In this exercise, players use their bodies to create a stage picture. The picture needs to capture a moment in the character's lives. We need to know what is going on in this moment just by looking at the arrangement of the player's bodies in space.

Get all the players to sit where they can see what is being created on stage. Give the group a word for inspiration. After the group gets the word, one player hops up on stage and creates a pose with their body. This player holds their pose. The rest of the group needs to take a moment and see what the first player created, then have another player add their body to the picture. Always take a moment to see what the players have created before another player is added. Keep adding bodies to the picture until it is complete. When the picture is complete, ask the players who are looking at it to come up with a title or caption for the stage picture.

This exercise will show your group the importance of "picturization" in scene work. In every scene we ever do, our bodies create a picture in space, and that picture communicates details about the characters and their relationship to each other. If the picture is created effectively, it will help tell the audience the meaning of this moment in the characters' lives. Once the players see how a stage picture can create meaning for what is happening in the scene, they will start to use this skill in their work.

After you introduce this exercise and the group gets the basic process down, talk about different visual elements the actors can use to compose their pictures. Here is a short list of visual elements:

Distance: the space between objects and bodies.
Shape: the shape our bodies make.
Levels: standing, seated, sitting on ground, lying on ground.
Focus: where the players are looking.
Emotion: the emotional feelings that manifest themselves in the body.

MOVING STAGE PICTURE

This is the same exercise as above, but now the players can move in the picture.

Here's how you do it:

The group gets a word, and then one player hops up on stage and creates a pose, movement, or gesture. If the player creates a movement or gesture, they must keep repeating it. The rest of the group needs to take a moment and see what the first player created, then have another player add their body to the picture by creating another pose, movement, or gesture. All movements must be repeated until the moving stage picture is complete. When the picture is complete, create a title or caption for it.

Special note about the stage picture and moving stage picture exercises: It's important for the players who are not in the picture to be in the audience rather than on a back line. The players looking at the picture will see the picture more clearly than the players in the picture. This will help the players see their scenes through the eyes of the audience, and therefore, they will create pictures that are more dynamic.

Another variation for these exercises is to create a stage picture or a moving stage picture and then start a scene after the picture is complete.

STAGE PICTURE: ROUND TWO (FIRST DATE, JOB INTERVIEW, OR BAD NEWS FROM THE DOCTOR)

In this exercise, the players use what they learned about picturization in the previous exercise to create a picture for the top of the scene.

Get two players on stage. The rest of the group poses the players on stage to create a stage picture. Put two chairs on stage so the characters can be seated if necessary. Make sure the stage picture is evocative enough to communicate something about how these characters relate to each other and the environment. The stage pictures that create tension work best.

After the picture is complete, tell the players on stage which one of three stock scenes to play—first date, job interview, or bad news from the doctor. I use these stock scene situations to show the effect a stage picture can have on a scene. A first date scene with the characters seated face-to-face will be completely different than a first date scene with the characters standing back-to-back.

Experience with the following visual elements is required to create effective stage pictures: distance, shape, levels, focus, and emotion (see previous page for definitions of these terms).

Chapter 19
Review of Steps 1–7

Before we get to the last step in my method to create awesome scenes, I wanted to take a moment and review the first seven steps.

Step 1: Getting connected with your partner or group

How to do it: Consciously shift your focus from self to other.

Step 2: *Yes and . . .*

How to do it: Harvest information, agree with what you harvested, and then add something based on what you got.

Step 3: The Pre-scene: The Five-Step Method and the Join

How to do it: The pre-scene, or the transformation into scene, has a first half and a second half. The first half of the pre-scene is a player, the beginner, using the five-step method to inspire an initial physical offer. The second half of the pre-scene is another player, the joiner, using the Join to somehow connect with the beginner.

Step 4: Building the Agreement: The Noodles

How to do it: At the top of a scene, after every offer is made, figure out what has been built, agree to it, and then make an offer that adds what has not been defined. Do that until all five scenic elements (character, relationship, environment, point of view, and point of attack) have been established and everyone in the scene knows what they are make-believing.

Step 5: Finding your Character's *How*: The Head, Heart, Body Method

How to do it: We know who your character is by what they do and the way they do it. That's what your character's *how* is—the way they do stuff. There are three ways into your character's *how*: your head, your heart, and your body.

With the Head method, you think of a character first, and then allow that thought to lead your transformation into that character.

With the Heart method, you drop into an emotional state first, and then allow that feeling to lead your transformation into character.

With the Body method, you explore movement, posture, gesture, and held tension first, and then allow how your body feels to lead your transformation into character.

Step 6: Making Environment Specific, Real, and Automatic: The Where-four

How to do it: Start every scene by defining any one of the Where-fours (placement, object, activity, or time), and then the domino effect kicks in, filling in the blanks. If you truly buy into one of the Where-fours, the other parts of the environment will start to take shape, and you will transform your environment into a real place. When you fully flesh out your environment, other scenic elements (character, relationship, point of view, and point of attack) are defined automatically.

Step 7: Adding the Sauce: Relationship and Point of View

How to do it: explore your character's point of view about the other character(s) in the scene in order to discover your Primary Emotional Drive.

You are looking for the one point of view your character has that gets more and more intense over time—the character's Primary Emotional Drive. Your character's Primary Emotional Drive needs to be focused on your scene partner.

After you discover your character's Primary Emotional Drive, you heighten it by employing the process of relationship. The process of relationship uses Relationship Components (history, emotion, status, physicality, space, and sensuality), or ways the characters are connected, to create cause and effect between the characters.

If you do steps 1 through 7, you will create good improv scenes. But if you want to be better than just good, if you want to create awesome improv scenes, you have to take it one more step. The final step in the "what to do, step-by-step, to create awesome scenes" method is believing in your world.

Improv is acting, and acting is believing.

But how do you learn to see the world through your character's eyes? How do you truly believe in the made-up world of the scene?

You use the three Method acting techniques I discussed in chapter 5—sense memory, emotional recall, and substitution.

Chapter 20
Step 8: Believing Your World

The Click

The Click, that moment when you feel your improviser brain relax and you start to have character thoughts, is the last step in my method to create awesome scenes. That's what we are working so hard for in steps 1 through 7—to build the world enough so you can see it through the eyes of your character. If you can truly see the world through your character's eyes, you will be able to do what 99 percent of improvisers cannot do—be a character instead of an improviser and believe in the scene you create.

I have seen a lot of improv, and honestly, I almost never see improvisers actually believe in what they create. It's understandable. Believing in your make-believe is difficult, but that's what separates truly awesome improvisers from just really good improvisers—acting. And remember, acting is believing.

I think believing in the made-up world of your scene is important, so how do you do it?

I use three basic techniques from Lee Strasberg's Method—sense memory, emotional recall, and substitution. I use these techniques to increase my belief in the world of the scene; but before we work on the nuts and bolts of how to use sense memory, emotional recall, and substitution, let's talk about something I call the *believe reflex*.

Humans are expert believers. Let's take you, for example. Why do you believe what is happening to you right now, this instant, in your real life?

Why is the experience of reading this book, wherever you are right now, real? What are you experiencing right now that proves to you that you are really reading this book?

Why are you an expert at believing your real life in the real world?

Because believing what is happening to you right now, this instant, in your real life is a reflex.

We humans have the believe reflex, and it works just like any other reflex—automatically. Like when a doctor hits your knee in exactly the right spot with a rubber hammer and your leg kicks up. A reflex works every time, as long as you get the right stimulus—as long as the rubber hammer hits just the right spot.

What stimulates your believe reflex?

Let's go back to some of those questions I just asked you.

Why do you believe what is happening to you right now? Why is the experience of reading this book, wherever you are right now, real? What is causing your believe reflex to kick in right now?

Two things: sensual experience and context/recognition. These two things are what stimulate the believe reflex in humans. If we can feel something with our five senses and recognize the context of that sensual stimulus from previous experience, then we believe it.

You believe you are reading this book right now because you can feel it in your hands and you can see the words on the page—you are being sensually stimulated. You also recognize this book and your environment from previous interactions with these things; that recognition gives you context for your behavior and makes you believe that it is real. You also know why you are reading this book. You have a reason for doing what you are doing, and that gives you even more context.

If you can't feel it and you don't recognize it, then you won't believe it.

If you recognize what you are doing, where you are doing it, and why you are doing it and you can feel it with your senses, then you believe it is real. That is the believe reflex, and you can trigger this impulse when you improvise.

How?

In order for the believe reflex to kick in, you need sensual stimulus and context/recognition. You need to feel what is going on with your five senses, and you need to be able to place what is going on into some kind of context. Recognizing what you are doing, where you are doing it, and why you are doing it creates context. I use the three basic techniques from Lee Strasberg's Method—sense memory, emotional recall, and substitution—to help create sensual stimulus and context in scenes.

Let's look at sense memory first.

Sense memory is when you remember a sensual experience from your real life in such detail that you reexperience the sensual stimuli. That's right, you recreate the experience; you relive it completely. You actually see things, hear things, and feel sensations. You don't just remember these things, you feel them again—in the present.

Think about sense memory as pantomime 2.0, where instead of just acting like you are holding a coffee cup, you feel the coffee cup in your hand—its weight, its texture . . . you even smell the coffee. You trick your brain into believing you are actually holding a coffee cup, even though you know you are not. Once you learn this skill, you can use sense memory in every scene you ever do. You can use it to experience the environment of the scene and help trigger the believe reflex. Below, you will find exercises that help you use sense memory to relive sensual experience.

SENSE MEMORY EXERCISES

The most important thing to understand when it comes to sense memory is that remembering a sensual experience is just the beginning of the technique. If you remember the sensual experience and stop short of reliving the experience, then this technique will not make you a better improviser. Sense memory only works if you can really feel the sensations from your past—in the present.

When using this technique, there are two keys to reexperiencing the sensation. First and foremost is the detail in which you remember the sensation from your past. No detail is too small when recalling a sensual experience, so when focusing on a memory, try to remember everything.

The second key to reexperiencing the sensation is participating with the thing causing the sensation. If you want to use sense memory to reexperience the sensation of splashing warm water on your face, then you need to participate with that water. You need to pantomime reaching into the sink, cupping your hands, and touching that water in order to really feel it. Sense memory is not just mental—it's physical. So, as you do these sense memory exercises, participate and interact with the thing that is causing the sensual stimulus. It will help tremendously with getting you to relive the sensation.

Also, it is unrealistic to expect success with sense memory the first time you try it. It takes some people years of practice before they actually reexperience the sensations from their sense memory. Try not to get discouraged; it took me a long time to be able to use the sense memory technique effectively. With enough practice, you can make sense memory automatic and increase your belief in your make-believe every time you improvise.

Here are three basic sense memory exercises. If you want more, there are hundreds of books about Strasberg's Method.

SENSE MEMORY EXERCISE: FLOATING IN WATER

Get the players to spread out in the space. Make sure everyone has enough room to move around as needed. Have everyone close their eyes and then ask them to remember the sensual experience of floating in water. Ask them how the water feels against their skin and how their body feels almost weightless in the water.

By now, you will see a miraculous transformation in the players. With their eyes closed, they will start to float. You will see their hands reach out to touch the water and their faces will relax, just as if they were really floating in water.

While they are floating, ask the players questions about their experience. I usually start with questions that isolate one sense at a time. Floating in water starts as a tactile sensation, so I start with questions that focus on the sense of touch. After the players start to reexperience the tactile sensation, I move on to questions about other senses.

Here are some sample questions:

What temperature is the water? (touch)
Can you touch the bottom or are you floating? (touch)
Is the water moving? (touch)
What can you see? (sight)
Where are you? Are you outside or inside? A bathtub? A pool? The ocean? A river? (sight)
Is it night or day? (sight)
What sounds can you hear? Running water, music, wildlife? (hearing)

After I have isolated a few senses with my questions and can see the players actually reexperiencing the sensation of floating in the water, I will ask them this:

Why are you in the water? What are you doing in the water?

This question helps the players contextualize the sensual experience and further stimulates their believe reflex.

After a few moments, get the players to open their eyes and ask how many of them actually felt the water on their skin. Usually, all of them do.

I always start with this sense memory because it gets the players to reexperience the feeling almost every time.

Why?

Because floating is a full-body experience and requires you to participate and interact with the thing that is causing the sensation. The success of this exercise is a great confidence builder for the players, and they are going to need it, because sense memory is hard to do.

SENSE MEMORY EXERCISE: SIGHT AND SOUND

Get the players to spread out in the space. Make sure everyone has enough room to move around as needed. Have everyone close their eyes, and then ask the players to remember someone who is important to them—someone who is still alive. Ask the players to see this person's face, their eyes, their hair, and every feature of this person's face. Encourage the players not to just remember this person's face, but to actually see it with their eyes closed.

With everyone's eyes closed, ask the players a few questions about their experience. Start with questions about what the players can see, and then move on to what they can hear.

Here are some sample questions:

What color are the person's eyes? (sight)
What color is their hair? (sight)
Do they have freckles on their skin? (sight)
Can you see the rest of this person's body? What clothes

are they wearing? (sight)
Where is this person—what environment or location? (sight)
Can you see this person move in their environment? (sight)
Can you hear this person speak? What are they saying? (hearing)
Is this person speaking to you? If so, what are they saying? (hearing)

After a few moments, get the players to open their eyes and ask how many of them could actually hear the person speak. Not everyone will be able to reexperience sound the first time they try. This exercise is harder than the first one because the goal is to reexperience two senses at the same time: sight and sound.

Strasberg stressed relaxation and concentration in his method. He believed you can't force a sense memory. You have to relax, concentrate on the details of the memory, and allow yourself to feel it. If a player can't reexperience their person's speech, have them return to reexperiencing the sight of their person. Have them see their person in greater detail, and that will help them eventually hear their person speak.

SENSE MEMORY EXERCISE: FAMILIAR OBJECT

Once again, have the players spread out in the space, making sure everyone has enough room to move around as needed. For this exercise, players do not close their eyes.

Ask the players to think of an object that they are familiar with, one that they know very well from their everyday life, like a cellphone or their favorite coffee mug. They need to remember this object completely—every aspect of this object. Its shape, color, texture, size, and weight.

After they have remembered the object in detail, ask them to see the object. They need to take their memory of this object and reexperience the sight of it.

After they see the object, ask them to touch the object. The goal is to actually feel the object with your hands.

A few tips: if you are having difficulty, you can do this exercise with your eyes closed first and then work up to doing it with your eyes open. You can start with touch and then move toward sight if that sequence works better for you.

Keep in mind that trying to remember a sensation in such detail that you feel it again in the present is very hard. It takes a lot of practice. Be honest with yourself; if you don't feel anything, relax, concentrate, and try again. Even if you feel just a small amount of sensation, remember that is a huge accomplishment.

If you start getting frustrated, return to the floating in water exercise to prove to yourself that you can actually reexperience a sensation. Keep your confidence up, and try to have a positive attitude, because negativity about your ability to use this technique will not make you better at doing it.

The Emotional Recall Technique

You need to be able to use the sense memory technique effectively enough to reexperience sensations before you try Emotional Recall.

Sense memory is powerful; you can use it to kick-start the believe reflex, you can use it to relive a sensual experience, but perhaps the most important use of sense memory is conjuring up emotions. When you remember and reexperience sensations you will often trigger an authentic emotional response.

Why?

Because you did not have that sensual experience in a vacuum. No, you experienced that sensation during your real life. You associate the sensation you are reliving with the real-life experiences that caused that sensation. If you relive the smell of your mom's Christmas cookies, you might tear up because the whole nostalgic memory comes flooding back. This connection between sensual experience and authentic emotion is something you can use—there is even a name for it; this process is called emotional recall or affective memory. I'm going to call it emotional recall from here on out.

Here is my description of how to use emotional recall (from chapter 5):

> . . . think of an event or experience in your real life that was emotionally profound, like when your dad hugged you after a big game or when your husband proposed to you. After you pick the event or experience, you use sense memory to recreate all the stimuli that were present. Here is the weird part: You do not focus on the emotions caused by the memory; you focus on the specific sensual experiences you felt during the event. You focus on these sense memories until they become real again and you reexperience them. It will be as if you were back in time, having the experience again. Then the authentic emotions will happen. You feel these emotions as a result of reexperiencing the sensual stimulus that was present during the memory, not by trying to feel a specific emotion.

It takes a lot of practice to master emotional recall, but once you use this technique to encounter a specific emotion, you will be able to tap into that feeling more easily in the future. You use the emotional recall process to discover your pathway to feeling a specific emotion. After you discover your pathway to an emotion, with practice, you can shorten the time it takes you to drop into that feeling. With enough practice you can create a library of emotions that you can tap into in an instant, because you have created an accessible pathway to that real feeling.

Let's look at emotional recall as a step-by-step process.

HOW TO USE EMOTIONAL RECALL

Step 1: Select an experience from your real life that was emotionally profound. Strasberg suggests using memories that are at least six years old; otherwise, the actor might be too affected by the memory to be able to control it.

Step 2: Recreate the sensual stimuli that were present during the experience. Take your time to go through each of the five senses one at a time. Make sure you are reexperiencing each sensation before you move onto the next sensation.

Step 3: Allow yourself to reexperience the event from your past. You know this is happening when it feels like you are back in time, having the experience again. You might be surprised by the emotion created by the memory—unhappy memories might make you laugh, and happy memories might make you cry. You won't know your emotional response to the memory until you have it. There is no right or wrong emotional response to the memory. You are just trying to cerate a pathway to an authentic emotion.

Step 4: Evaluate what emotion was created in response to the emotional recall process, and repeat steps 1–3 to see if you can get the same results again and again.

SOME TIPS WHEN USING EMOTIONAL RECALL

Use memories that are at least six years old. You are looking for memories that you care deeply about, but not stuff that is going to put you in therapy.

Work through each sense, one at a time, making sure that you are reexperiencing one sense before you move onto the next sense. You will find a sequence that works for you. It is normal for you to be better at reexperiencing one sense than another. You might be great at seeing things, but not very good at hearing things. Start with the sense you are good at; then move on to the senses that are harder for you to reexperience.

The goal is to reexperience all the specific sensations that were present during your event.

If a specific emotional recall gets different results each time you do it, then discard it. You are looking for consistent results from your emotional recall.

When you find an emotional recall that consistently works to create a specific emotion, do it over and over again. Eventually, you will be able to drop into this emotion in the blink of an eye.

Emotional recall creates a pathway to a specific emotion. You can use that pathway to drop into that emotion authentically and automatically. The more pathways you develop, the more emotions you can access in scenes.

The Substitution Technique

Now that you have mastered emotional recall to the point that you can automatically drop into any emotion in an instant, you are ready to use emotional recall to fuse your emotions onto your character during scenes. The process of fusing your real emotions about events in your real life onto your character is called substitution, and it works to increase belief in the world of the scene.

Let's say your partner initiates a scene about a sick pet that your character loves very much. This dramatic situation requires your character to feel sadness about their sick pet, but right now, in this moment, you are not sad at all. You are actually kind of happy because you are getting to do some improv. In this scene, you have two choices. You could fake it and act sad. Y'know, you could do all the stuff that sad people do, like frown and cry, or you could use substitution to authentically feel some sadness.

Let me just state for the record that most of the time I just fake it. I pretend. I make-believe that I am sad or happy or scared, whatever the scene demands. I make-believe that I feel the emotion, and then after a few moments, I start to actually feel it, but this is only because I have used the sense memory and emotional recall techniques so many times that they have become automatic. I don't even have to think about doing these techniques anymore—I can just drop into an emotion.

The substitution technique is for those times when faking it does not work. Sometimes there is a moment in a scene that requires you to be sad or happy or scared and you just can't hit that note. That's when you use substitution.

Here is how you would use substitution to feel sadness in the scene about your character's sick pet.

Step 1: Choose the emotion you are trying to create. In this case, it would be sadness.

Step 2: Drop into an emotional recall that creates that specific emotion in you. (See the step-by-step process for emotional recall on page 213.)

Step 3: Feel that authentic emotion.

Step 4: Switch the make-believe sick pet for the real event from your emotional recall.

Now, instead of feeling sad about the event from your real life, your character will feel sad about their sick pet. You will be feeling authentic emotions about the event from your real life, but you will focus those emotions on your make-believe world. When you do this, you will have fused your real feelings to the character.

When you fuse your real feelings to the character, your belief in the world of the scene skyrockets. You will believe the world of the scene because you are putting some of your real life into it. Substitution is a powerful technique to create the Click, and it can stimulate the believe reflex because it grafts a context from your real life onto the scene.

In my experience, the more I use sense memory, emotional recall, and substitution, the better I get at being able to drop into any situation. I drop in so fast, I can't even tell if I am just make-believing or actually using substitution. It does not matter what method you use to get there as long as you end up in the same place—believing in your world.

Substitution Exercises

Actually, I have used substitution a couple of times already in this book. Let me show you.

In the "Scene Painting: Real Place" exercise in chapter 17, the players describe an environment from their real life and then do a scene in that environment. In that exercise, the players substitute a real place for the made-up place of the scene. When you treat the environment of the scene like a place from your real life, you increase your belief in the world.

Why?

Because you are starting the scene by visualizing a real place, and that means you are starting the scene with a sensual experience. You also have a context for the environment because you recognize it from your real life. Sensual experience and context/recognition trigger the believe reflex. If you can see and recognize your environment, you will automatically believe the world of the scene.

Another example of substitution is in the "Imagined Past: Real Person" exercise on page 173. In that exercise, a player treats their scene partner in the same way they treat a person from their real life. They are substituting a real person for their scene partner's made-up character in the scene.

You can substitute anything from your real life into a scene to increase belief in the world. Here are three more substitution exercises to try. Make sure you have experience with the basic four-step substitution process outlined in the previous chapter before you try these exercises.

BEGINNER STARTS WITH SUBSTITUTION

Two players on stage—player A (the beginner) and player B (the joiner).

Player A does an emotional recall in order to drop into an authentic emotional state. Player A will stay in this emotional state for the duration of the scene.

While player A is in their emotional state, give him/her an input word and allow them to go through the five-step method to begin a scene. The player's emotional state will influence their cascade, and that is completely normal.

Player A makes an initial physical offer (in their emotional state), player B joins player A's initial offer, and the scene starts. Player B can play any emotion they want.

If player A is doing their emotional recall correctly, they will be experiencing authentic emotions. During the scene, these emotions become the character's emotions. The goal of this exercise is for player A to stay emotionally connected throughout the scene and to feel their emotions about the make-believe world rather than their real life. You may have to remind player A that they are playing a character in the scene and not themselves.

That is what substitution is—making your character feel your real emotions. But remember, the character has these feelings about their world, not your world. If your emotional recall is about the excitement you felt when you won your first soccer game, all we want is the excitement, not the soccer game. You character feels the excitement about what is happening in the scene, not about the soccer game from your past. You just use the past event to get to the authentic feelings, and then you fuse those feelings to your character.

Some Tips

Give player A plenty of time to go through their emotional recall.

Warn the players that this exercise can be emotionally demanding. People might actually cry. They might get upset or angry, and that is all part of emotional recall. In order to be able to play these emotions on stage, you have to be able to really feel them as a person.

Make sure player A's emotional recall is complete before you give them an input word. An emotional recall is only complete when the player is fully dropped into an emotional state.

Player A is not playing himself/herself in the scene. Make sure his/her character and environment are not coming from their emotional recall. Player A's character and environment need to come from their cascade in the five-step method, not their real-life memory. This separation is tricky for some players.

This exercise can blow up in your face because the players are using real emotions. Just be aware that not every improviser is comfortable being emotionally vulnerable. Respect everyone's individual process, but try not to make this exercise into a therapy session. Emotional recall and substitution are acting techniques and are not intended to help people deal with difficult experiences from their past. If you or someone in your group can't use emotional recall without getting upset, then stop doing it. Really. No kidding.

JOINER STARTS WITH SUBSTITUTION

Two players on stage—player A (the beginner) and player B (the joiner).

Player B does an emotional recall in order to drop into an authentic emotional state. Player B will stay in this emotional state for the duration of the scene.

While player B is in their emotional state, give player A an input word and allow them to go through the five-step method to start a scene.

Player A makes their initial physical offer, and player B (in their emotional state) joins. Player A speaks first to start the scene. Player A can play any emotion they want.

In this scene, it is player B's job to feel their authentic emotion about whatever player A initiates at the top of the scene. The key is that player B really feels their emotions before the scene starts, and then focuses that feeling toward player A at the top of the scene. Whatever player A establishes at the top of the scene becomes the motivation for player B's emotional state.

This will create a strong cause and effect at the top of the scene. Player B will be feeling his/her feeling because of what player A does and says at the top of the scene. Allow the players to explore their character's point of view and see where the scene goes.

The goal of this exercise is for player B to stay emotionally connected throughout the scene and to feel their emotions about the make-believe world rather than their real life. These scenes can become heated because this exercise requires player B to be feeling their emotion about player A's initial offer. These scenes can start heightening very quickly.

Emotional recall and substitution are acting techniques and are not intended to help people deal with difficult experiences from their past. If you or someone in your group can't use emotional recall without getting upset, then stop doing it. Really. No kidding.

Some Tips

Give player B plenty of time to go through their emotional recall.

Warn the players that this exercise can be emotionally demanding. People might actually cry. They might get upset or angry, and that is all part of emotional recall. In order to be able to play these emotions on stage, you have to be able to really feel them as a person.

Make sure player B's emotional recall is complete before you give player A an input word. An emotional recall is only complete when the player is fully dropped into an emotional state.

SPONTANEOUS SUBSTITUTION

Two players on stage—player A and player B.

Player A does an emotional recall in order to drop into an authentic emotional state. Player A does not stay in this emotional state for the duration of the scene; they wait until they are motivated in the scene to drop into their emotional state. It is as if player A is loading this emotion into a gun so he/she can shoot it whenever they want.

Player A releases this emotional state.

Give both players an input word and allow them to go through the five-step method to start a scene.

Either player can make the initial physical offer. After one player makes the initial physical offer, it is joined by the remaining player.

The scene starts, and the players build their agreement. At some point during the scene, player B does something that motivates player A to drop into his/her loaded emotion.

The goal is not for player A to play the emotion, but to truly drop into the authentic feeling from their emotional recall. That's what substitution is—taking your real feelings about an event from your real life and fusing them to your character. And improvisers need to be able to do this spontaneously.

You need to be able to spontaneously substitute any emotion from your real life onto your character whenever you feel motivated to do so. This exercise is designed to teach you that skill.

Chapter 21
Micro-techniques

Okay, you have gone through my eight steps to create awesome scenes, but I have a few more methods to share. I promised I would share with you what I call my *micro-techniques*. Here is a refresher on micro-techniques from earlier in the book:

> Through repetition and years of trial and error, I created a bunch of what I call *micro-techniques* to help me be a better improviser. Where another improviser would use their talent, I would develop a micro-technique. I would seem like I was this great improviser who was super-talented, but in reality, I had just trained myself to use a micro-technique. Use a micro-technique enough times and it becomes second nature—you forget you are even using it. Create enough micro-techniques, and you will seem awesome and talented, but really, you will just be well trained.

So, a micro-technique is a simple, easy to use, step-by-step process that I bring into play during a scene. I use these techniques in order to have more success in the scenes I create. Here is a list of the micro-techniques I use, how to do them, and why I think they are helpful:

Talk about what you are doing so you don't have to talk about what you are doing.

Talking about what you are doing in a scene gets a bad wrap. I have been told hundreds of times "Don't talk about what you are doing." Improv teachers love to tell you what not to do. I think telling improvisers not to talk about what they are doing is crazy advice to give actors who have to create a scene without costumes, props, or scenery. Sometimes you have to tell your partner what you are pantomiming so they know what you are creating in the scene. I look at it this way—I might as well tell you I am frosting your birthday cake because you might think I'm stabbing a cat.

Remember, the goal at the top of the scene is to get everyone on the same page so we can move forward with that information. If I just go ahead and tell my partner what I'm doing at the top of the scene, then lots of scenic elements are going to be established and we are going to get to play inside the agreement that much faster.

The problem with this approach is when your partner takes the opportunity to tell you that what you're doing is wrong. If I tell my scene partner I am frosting their birthday cake, and then he/she starts to argue with me about the fact that I'm using the wrong flavor of frosting, we are in trouble. I am not telling my partner what I am doing to start a fight—I am letting her know we are in a world where characters frost cakes. How about a little *yes and*?

I talk about what I am doing as a way to make my initial offer clear to everyone in the scene. Improvisers are not magicians. We cannot read each other's minds, so we might as well share what we are doing as clearly as possible, and sometimes that requires that you talk about what you are doing. It is a way to clearly establish the world of the scene. Then we can move onto deeper, more important stuff that the character cares about.

Character match

When I use this micro-technique, I match whatever *how* my scene partner plays at the top of the scene. I do whatever I am doing in the scene the same way my partner is doing what they are doing. If they are really fired up about everything, then so am I. If they talk in a British accent, then so do I. I do not have to be the same type of character they are—if they are an overly emotional, damsel in distress, I can still be Prince Charming. I just will be a Prince Charming that matches my partner's overly emotional damsel-in-distress way of doing things.

But honestly, most of the time when I do a character match, I play a very similar character to that of my partner. When my partner plays a good ol' boy sitting on a stump, strummin' on a banjo, I play a good ol' boy sitting on a stump, sawin' on a fiddle—a character match. I do this automatically without even thinking about it.

The character match doubles the power of the first player's choice and creates an automatic connection between the characters.

This is kind of like _____, so I will make it more like _____.

Lots of times in a scene, the players are in an underdefined world. Sure, we know a few things about the world, but not quite enough to really sink our teeth into it. This is a technique for those moments in scenes when you kind of know what is going on, but it would be a lot more fun if you just knew completely.

Let's say I am in a scene and thinking, "Hey, this is kind of like a bank robbery," so I will make it more like a bank robbery by doing something that one does during a bank robbery. If I am in a scene and thinking, "Hey, it's kind of like we are in an English garden playing badminton," I will make it more like that. We usually don't know what we are going to create before we start doing it, so I try to figure out what we are doing is kind of like and then I make it more like that.

This works for pretty much any scenic element (character, relationship, environment, point of view, or point of attack) that is underdefined.

If I got nothing, I do nothing.

If I have no clue what is going on in the scene, I do nothing until I figure out something that I can agree to. This happens at least once in almost every scene I ever do.

I have found that an improviser's usual response to having no clue what is going on is to talk and move as much as possible, but this just creates more confusion. If I have no clue what is going on, I just wait, watch, and listen; I use other-focus to find something I can *yes and* in the scene.

This sounds easy, but when you're faced with not knowing anything in the scene, it is very hard to just do nothing. However, sometimes doing nothing is the best thing.

Stop talking the moment someone else starts talking.

This micro-technique is short and sweet: the moment someone else starts talking, I stop talking. I cannot talk and listen at the same time, so unless it is a character/relationship choice to interrupt or talk over my partner, I always stop talking when they start. I also ask my partner to do the same for me.

This is especially true at the top of a scene when the players are trying to define their world. It is too easy to miss an important piece of information if you talk at the same time as your partner.

But like I said before, it is totally valid to make a character or relationship choice that leads you to interrupt or talk over your partner—just make sure it is not an improviser choice.

Touch something on the downstage wall.

Some of these micro-techniques are just little tricks to give you a few more seconds to figure out what you are make-believing. This is one of those "little trick" micro-techniques. If I have nothing in a scene, if I am truly drawing a blank, I walk to the downstage wall and touch an imaginary object. If you don't have a background in theatre, the downstage wall is sometimes called the fourth wall; it is the invisible wall that separates the characters from the audience. It is the wall that would be there if the scene was happening in a real room.

So, I will walk to a specific place on the downstage wall, reach out with my hand, and grab something without knowing what that thing is. I will just grab something that is on the imaginary counter. My hands will start to pantomime; and by touching this imaginary object, I will discover what it is. Here is the important part: I discover what the object is by touching it, not by thinking. My hands tell my head what the object is, and then I know something about the world of the scene. Once I know I am holding a baseball mitt or a pot of chicken soup or a cellphone, I start to make a series of other discoveries about who I am and where I am.

I have found that once you know one thing, you start to know everything by using the domino effect . . . and that is the next micro-technique.

The domino effect

This micro-technique is all over this book. I use the domino effect every time I improvise. Here is the basic micro-technique that can be applied in a ton of different ways: make one choice—any choice, like touching something on the downstage wall or a funny walk or the idea that your character is a cowboy or that you are driving a car—really, any choice about anything in the scene. Then allow that specific choice to inspire the next obvious choice. And by obvious choice, I mean whatever is obvious to you. If you make a choice and nothing seems obvious, I would suggest that you are either being too clever or you are afraid that your next choice won't make the audience laugh.

What this micro-technique does for me is that every choice I make automatically inspires the next discovery. The key is to keep the focus inside the make-believe world—then discoveries are easy to make. If you start to listen to the audience or judge your scene, then there will be too much space between the dominoes and one will fall without touching the next domino.

If you concentrate on the world of the scene, each piece of reality that you create automatically leads you to the discovery of the next piece of the reality.

Start in the middle.

"Start the scene in the middle" is a classic improv mantra, but how do you actually start in the middle? I have always had a hard time doing it. Everyone I knew had a hard time doing it. I know it's an effective way to throw a ton of assumed information out there and see what happens, but I just was not that good at it. When I tell myself to "start in the middle," I get nothing. So, I broke "starting in the middle" into its parts. I thought, "What do I do to start in the middle?" I wanted to know how to start in the middle. I realized that starting in the middle meant that there was a beginning that happened before the start of the scene. Thinking about the middle never helped me create the middle. I had to think about the moment before the middle that created my need to respond.

So, I created a short two-step process. First, I pick something specific that just happened to my character, and then I react to it. "Starting in the middle" just means something happened before the audience gets to watch. The characters didn't start in the middle—the characters started in the beginning, and we just picked up their story in the middle. If my first line is a reaction to something that just happened, then I am in the middle of the scene.

Here are some examples of first lines that respond to something specific:

(A waiter just brought your food.) "The pasta with red sauce looks delicious."

(A co-worker just asked you out on a date.) "Shannon, I'm flattered, but I'd like to keep our relationship professional."

(The boss just called.) "Hey, Jack, the boss just called and I covered for you."

In these three examples, I am selecting something specific that just happened and responding to it in character. It seems like I am talented at "starting in the middle," but really, I'm not—I'm just doing a micro-technique. I'm simply responding to a specific that just happened.

Breathe in the other person's line.

I have been using this technique since I was a teenager in acting school. It's an old scripted acting trick that I use in improv all the time. Here is how you do it: While your scene partner is talking, breathe in what they are saying—literally. Take a breath in as they talk.

There are two major benefits to breathing in your partner's line. First, it will keep you from talking when they speak, since you can't chatter while you breathe in. This is a huge positive because if two people are talking at the same time, no one is listening. Second, you will be taking their line of dialogue into your body with your breath. You are more apt to be affected by what your partner says if you take it in with your breath.

More often than not, you will breathe in your partner's line and breathe out your response. This back and forth follows the natural rhythm of how humans converse and will feel like you are really talking with your partner.

Momentum

In mathematics, momentum is the mass of an object multiplied by its velocity. That's how I think about this micro-technique. In my improv-momentum equation, the mass is my scene partner and the velocity is their point of view.

When I use momentum, I first assess the point of view of my scene partner. I do that by filling in the blanks of the following statement: "My partner feels _____ about _____." Once I figure out that "my partner feels *angry* about *getting a speeding ticket*" or "*excited* about *their upcoming vacation*" or whatever, I actively do stuff to make them feel that way more. I increase their velocity, therefore increasing their momentum. All I am doing is pushing them in the direction they are already going. This works if the point of view is about the dramatic situation, themself, or you—you just need to figure out what they are feeling and make them feel it more.

Be the reason why.

This technique is kind of like the momentum trick, because it requires assessing your partner's point of view by filling in the blanks of the statement "My partner feels _____ about _____." Once I figure out how my partner feels about what is going on in the scene, I become the reason my partner is feeling their feeling. If they are angry about getting a speeding ticket, I tell them I saw the cop car in plenty of time to warn them but chose not to. Now I have become the reason they are angry. If they are excited about their upcoming vacation, I let them know that I'm the one who approved their time off work. Now I have become the reason they are excited. I make my character the cause of their feeling.

Being the reason why your partner is feeling their feeling automatically puts the two of you in a cause-and-effect relationship. It is the easiest and most direct way to make your partner feel their point of view—more. It adds momentum to your partner's point of view and creates an easy path to heightening.

I feel ____ because ____.

This micro-technique is another one that utilizes the domino effect to go from knowing one small piece of information about your character to knowing everything. I feel ____ because ____ is a simple process of dropping into an emotional state first and then allowing the emotional state to tell you why you are feeling it. The moment you know why you feel the way you feel, lots of other information about the scene is defined.

Here is how you do it: At the top of a scene you spontaneously and authentically drop into an emotion. As you start to feel the emotion, other specific information about the character's world will take shape, you will begin to visualize the environment, and then you will spontaneously know why you are feeling your emotion. If you want, you can start the scene by making the statement "I feel ____ because ____."

I am sweeping, so I am a janitor.

I like to start scenes with an activity. I like how effectively doing something and touching stuff helps create the environment. With this micro-technique, I start with an activity and let it tell me who I am in the scene. I spontaneously start a scene with an activity. I just reach out, touch an imagined object, and start doing something with it. For example, I might reach out and grab a broom, so I will start sweeping. As I am doing the activity, I ask myself the question, "What kind of character sweeps?" Then whatever character pops in my head is what I transform into. I literally think, "I am sweeping; a janitor sweeps, so I'll be a janitor." Knowing that my character is a janitor helps me make many more choices. It gets the domino effect going and leads to a series of discoveries about the world of the scene.

With this micro-technique, you really have to allow the activity to tell you who you are instead of the other way around. This technique is for when you are not inspired to create a specific character but still find yourself in a scene.

The awesome thing about this technique is that you can get several different character ideas from the same activity. This time, sweeping led me to janitor; next time, it might lead me to some other piece of information about who I am. The key is that each piece of information leads you to the next piece of information, one domino at a time.

Emotional pantomime or Object to event

This micro-technique kind of combines the last two. I take the idea that an object or a pantomime can define a character and add the fact that if I just drop into an emotional state, I will spontaneously know why I am feeling that way.

Here is how I do it: I start a scene by visualizing an object. I make sure I can really see the object, and then I touch it and start to do something with it. After that, as I am pantomiming with the imagined object, I spontaneously add an emotional state.

It might go something like this: I visualize a bowling ball. I go over and touch the bowling ball. I pick it up and start shining it. I add the emotional state of sadness. I then discover I am shining my dead friend's bowling ball as I get ready to go bowl in the big tournament. That is a pretty big moment in my character's life. We were on this bowling team together, and it was my friend's dream to use this ball in the tournament finals. I decide that, as a tribute to my dead friend, I will use his bowling ball in the finals. As I put my dead friend's bowling ball in its case, I can barely hold back tears because I want so badly for him to be here right now.

The object of bowling ball led me to the event in my character's life where I pay tribute to my dead friend. I discovered all this by making one small choice followed by a series of discoveries. This technique can help you discover why your character does what they do. It can spontaneously reveal your character's inner life.

Get hurt instead of mad.

This micro-technique operates on the theory that one bad guy is enough in a scene. When my partner does something that my character doesn't want them to do, I always consider getting hurt rather than getting mad. That way, we don't have two jerks in the scene. If my scene partner does something jerky to me and I do something jerky to him/her, then everyone in the scene is a jerk and the audience doesn't know who they're supposed to care about. And I have got some news for you—if the audience doesn't care about any of the characters, we are in big trouble.

We want our improv to be filled with characters that are affected by what happens to them during the scene, and you have to be vulnerable in order to be affected. Audiences care about the characters that change—characters who are affected by their world—and being vulnerable helps you do that. Getting mad is a way to keep yourself from being vulnerable. It is a way to protect yourself. Why protect your vulnerability when you can explore it and heighten it?

Like your scene partner's character, or be like your scene partner's character.

I use this micro-technique if I don't have a strong idea about what I am trying to do at the top of a scene, which is at least half the time because I like to start scenes with a join and just see what happens.

If I am joining the beginner at the top of the scene, I try to either like or be like my scene partner's character. This like-or-be-like mindset can counteract some of the panic that is a natural response to not knowing anything at the top of a scene.

Here is how you like your partner: At the top of the scene, when your partner does something, go ahead and be okay with them doing it, unless you have darn a good reason to not be okay with what they are doing.

But what do you do when your partner is doing something your character does not like?

If you do have a good reason to not like what your partner is doing, then consider matching their *how* or, as I say, be like them.

That way, even though you are in conflict with your partner, you at least have something in common—you are a little alike. In fact, the more the characters are alike, the more conflict the audience will tolerate, especially at the top of the scene.

I'm not saying don't explore conflict when you improvise—there are no rules and no *don't*s in this book—what I am saying is that you should earn the conflict by knowing why you don't like what your partner is doing. For me, if I am just joining my partner at the top of a scene, I assume that what my partner is doing is right for this situation. If my partner is trimming the hedges, I just figure that is what he's supposed to be doing at the top of the scene. That is, unless my partner lets me know that what they are doing is inappropriate for the situation; then I support them by objecting.

So, at the top of the scene, I align myself with my partner. I either like them or am like them.

No defense

This is a Keith Johnstone technique. I just like it and use it so much that I wanted to include it in my list.

If my partner accuses me of doing something wrong, instead of defending myself, I admit to everything. If they say I borrowed their car without asking, I admit to it immediately and reveal the fact that I got in a fender bender while I was out. If they say I'm late to work, instead of arguing about how hard I work and the sacrifices I have made for the company, I apologize for being late and admit to regularly stealing pens from the office supply closet.

No defense does two things. First, it aggressively *yes and*s what you have been given by your partner, and second, it jump-starts the heightening process. If my partner is already upset that I'm late to work, how are they going to feel about me stealing all those pens? They are going to get more upset. That sounds a lot like momentum to me, and I think pushing characters in the direction that they are already headed is a good thing.

When in doubt, repeat.

Here is how I put it to my students: I walk backward through scenes. I am not thinking about what happens next; I am thinking about how can I bring back the stuff I have already created. I love to repeat myself and look at it as an opportunity to communicate to the world the type of person my character is.

So, when I can't think of the next thing to do or say in the scene (and this happens all the time), I repeat something I have already done or said. I pour myself another glass of sweet tea, I get another place setting to put on the table, I do something I have already done—again. It reminds me of who I am and keeps me connected with the make-believe world.

Sounds before words

I love to make nonverbal sounds at the top of the scene, before I speak, to start the domino effect for my character. Nonverbal sounds like laughter and crying are a great way to find who you are in the scene. I will start making a sound, then figure out what feeling or thought is behind it. Once I discover what is behind the sound, I let the domino effect lead me to a series of discoveries about my character and world.

Character passion/obsession

This micro-technique is about making a bold choice at the top of a scene and letting the chips fall where they may. In fact, that is a great way to approach any scene—make a strong choice and see what develops.

With this micro-technique, the bold choice I make is my character's passion or obsession. I choose a passion or obsession for my character at the top of the scene and see how that starts the domino effect of other choices and discoveries. I promise, if you decide that your character has a passion about Civil War reenactments, you will automatically know a bunch of other things about your character. That one bold choice kick-starts the domino effect and fills in so many blanks about your character.

If you know one thing about your character, you can know

everything about your character, and it helps if that one thing you know is important to your character. What could be more important than your passion or obsession?

Micro-techniques covered earlier in the book:

A lot of the exercises I outlined earlier in the book can also be used as micro-techniques during scenes. Here is a list of the exercises from earlier in the book (with page numbers) that I think work great as micro-techniques.

Start with the Join. (Pages 34–45)

The Join is the most important micro-technique that I use. I use it every time I do a scene. I think making the Join automatic is the most important thing to learn for any person who is just starting out. I think of the Join as *yes and*-ing with my body. Most of the time when I am lost at the top of a scene, it's because I was focused on myself instead of my partner and skipped the most important step to starting a scene: the Join.

Start by establishing a scenic element. (Pages 138–145)

This is what I am doing at the top of every scene—building the agreement, one scenic element at a time. If you initiate a scene by establishing a scenic element, you are starting strong and giving your partner something they can hold onto.

Start by using the Head, Heart, Body method to transform into character. (Pages 146–157)

After you spend some time with the Head, Heart, Body method, you can use it to initiate scenes. You can start a scene by knowing something about yourself and allow the domino effect to create a transformation—that's the head. You can start a scene in an emotional state and allow the domino effect to create a transformation—that's the heart. Or you can start with movement, posture, and/or held tension and allow the domino effect to create a transformation—that's the body.

Making a head, heart, and/or body choice at the top of a scene is a micro-technique I use every time I do a scene.

Start by establishing a Relationship Component. (Pages 168–200)

Relationship components are ways characters can be connected. They are history, emotion, status, physicality, space, and sensuality. You can start scenes by establishing one or more of these components at the top of a scene. It's a risky approach because Relationship Components tend to create tension and conflict between the characters, but it sure is fun to jump-start the cause and effect right at the top of a scene.

Start with a sensual experience. (Pages 50–52 and 206–211)

Starting a scene with a sensual experience is the most powerful way to establish your environment. Experiencing the world through your senses stimulates the believe reflex, making the world of the scene real for you and believable to the audience. To be able to start scenes with a sensual experience, you have to master the sense memory technique outlined earlier in the book. Remember, sense memory is not just the memory of a sensual experience—it is the reliving of the sensual experience.

To use the micro-technique of starting scenes with a sensual experience, it's not enough just to say that you are feeling a sensation. You have to be able to really feel an imagined sensation.

Chapter 22
Long Form or Short Form? No Need to Pick One

There used to be this heated debate about long-form and short-form improv. Improvisers used to argue about which one created a better show and which one was more pure as an art form. Improvisers were divided into these two camps—long formers and short formers. If you were a long former, you looked down on short form for pandering to the audience's desire to be entertained. If you were a short former, you criticized long form for being pretentious and self-indulgent.

Well, it seems to me that in recent history, long form has won the debate.

Why do I think that?

If you live in New York City, Chicago, or Los Angeles, you are watching and performing long form. If you travel to these big cities to take improv classes at the established improv theatres, you are going to be taught how to do long form. If you go to an improv festival anywhere in the country, the vast majority of the improv teams and groups are going to be doing long form. And, currently, the biggest names in the field of improv are performing and teaching long form.

It seems to me that the debate is over and the people have voted with their feet. Improvisers are choosing to do long form. The problem with this picture is that audiences prefer short form, especially in small-to-midsized cities and towns across America. I know I am generalizing, but I'll say it again: Audiences like short form, and improvisers like long form.

There is an inherent solution to this problem—do both, and do them well.

There is no need to pick between long-form and short-form improv. At Theatre 99, where I teach and perform, we do both. We do a hybrid show. We do an act of scenic short-form improv, take an intermission, and then we do an act of long-form improv. The performers prefer doing the long form, and the audience prefers the short form, so everyone gets what they want.

Why do audiences prefer short form?

Because they know what it is. Millions of people have seen *Whose Line Is It Anyway?*, and relatively few people even know what long-form improv is. Most people have never seen a live improv show, not to mention a long-form improv show. So, even though improv as an art form is moving toward long form, most people's only exposure to improv is short-form improv games played on *Whose Line Is It Anyway?* The general public is not known for taking chances; they like to do and see stuff they have done and seen before. Short form is also more easily understood and allows for more audience participation.

This fact may not matter to you. You may just love doing improv and don't care about developing an audience for your show. It depends on what you want as an improviser. If your goals are purely artistic, and you just want to do the type of improv that you like best, then do that. But if you want to create an improv group with mainstream appeal that performs for large audiences, then you might want to include some short-form improv in your show. What I am saying is that there is no need to choose—you can have the best of both worlds by doing both types of improv.

For me, the style of improv (long or short form) does not matter. All that matters is that the scenes I create with my partners have integrity. By "integrity," I mean that the players are focused on the goal of creating a made-up world that everyone can believe in. That is all that matters to me—scenic integrity, regardless of whether I am doing a two-minute short-form game or a half-hour long-form set.

Long form or short form, it's all just spontaneous, make-believe scenes created by the players. Improv, long form or short form, is acting, and acting is believing. The moment I stop believing my world and start trying to make the audience laugh is when I lose my integrity. It is the scenic integrity of the work that is important, not the length of it.

I do not think long form inherently has more integrity than short form, but you do have to be more vigilant when you are doing short-form games; otherwise, you can start just going for the laugh. I always try to keep in mind that the scene is more important than the game or the form.

With scenic integrity in mind, I would like to say I enjoy both long-form and short-form improv for different reasons, and I am an advocate for cross training. I think doing both long-form and short-form improv will make you better at both.

Why?

Because they work different muscles, or, as I say, "In long form, you discover, and in short form, you deliver."

Long form requires that you discover, through exploration with your partner, what is awesome about the world of the scene. There is a purity to long form because you are free to discover without a bunch of manipulation by the audience. Typically, in long form, the audience does not get to influence the performance after some kind of initial suggestion. The players are free to play. Depending on the type of long form you are doing, there are very few rules, so you can basically do anything you want.

This playful discovery is what I love about long form. Because you have time to explore and are not forced to play a predetermined game, long-form scenes are more organic. You have no clue where the humor is going to come from—it is just you and your partner up there without a plan. The only way you are going to succeed is by connecting, cooperating, and believing in your world. This focus on partnership and discovering the world together in long-form improv will strengthen your technique.

Short form requires that you quickly deliver scenic elements in order for a game to be layered over the scene. There is a precision to short form because the games often have strict rules that must be followed during the scene. In short form, the players have to be proficient at creating strong, concrete scenic agreements often dictated by an audience suggestion. Short form players need to establish the *who, what, where* at the top of the scene because, often, the gimmick of the game works against the scene. In fact, most short-form improv games make it harder to believe in the world of the scene.

That is what I love about short form: the challenge. You can get a short-form scene wrong because the games usually have rules. To succeed at short form, you have to learn how to do two things at once. You have to play the scene and the game simultaneously, and delivering strong, concrete scenic elements at the top of the scene makes that so much easier. This focus on establishing concrete beginnings of scenes in short-form improv will strengthen your technique.

So, long form will teach you how to be free, and short from will teach you discipline. Without discipline, there is no freedom. Without freedom, discipline is worthless.

Do both long and short form, and you will learn both freedom and discipline.

Chapter 23
Me, Theatre 99, and How to Get Improv to Love You Back

I knew I wanted to do improv for the rest of my life in 1986 when, at age 18, I took an improv workshop at the International Thespian Conference at Ball State University in Muncie, Indiana. During that workshop, I did an improv scene where I completely lost myself in my character. I was not myself in the scene—I was the character—and it felt amazing. I had never heard of the instructor and can't even remember his name. I was just curious about improv and wanted to try it. As I walked out of that workshop, I literally heard a voice in my head say, "I want to do that with my life."

So, I have.

Since then, I have done thousands of shows and still feel pure joy when I lose myself in a scene and see the world through my character's eyes. In 1995, I cofounded The Have Nots! Improv Comedy Company with Brandy Sullivan, and less than a year later, we were joined by Timmy Finch. In 2000, Brandy, Timmy, and I built our own theatre in the heart of beautiful downtown Charleston, South Carolina, and we named it Theatre 99.

Building our own brick-and-mortar theatre changed everything. Building a theatre meant I was putting down roots—I was committing to Charleston and giving up the dream that one day I would move to New York City and "make it." I started teaching a Sunday evening drop-in class, and eventually, with Brandy's encouragement, I created the curriculum taught in Theatre 99's improv training program. Eventually, I found a new dream: I wanted to give my students the same life-changing experience I had been given years before in that workshop taught by that guy whose name I can't remember, and for some, I have.

Since day one, Theatre 99 has been dedicated to producing world-class improv shows for audiences who like to laugh. The people who come to see our shows are not improv comedy fans—they are just regular people who want to have a good time. The type of improv we do is accessible—you don't have to even know what improv is to enjoy our shows. We do both short-form and long-form improv, but the audience just sees it all as spontaneous scenes created by the actors. I am proud of the fact that we at Theatre 99 have made going to a live improv show as normal as going out for dinner and a movie—at least for people who live in Charleston.

I have been teaching improv for over 20 years, but it's in the last 10 years, at Theatre 99, where I have had the chance to develop the ideas outlined in this book. Hundreds of students have gone through Theatre 99's training program, and I have had the chance to adapt my approach based on their success. I learned how to teach by teaching. If an exercise worked, I kept doing it; if it did not, I stopped. The step-by-step methods and exercises in this book are the ones that worked.

The result of a decade of classes taught at Theatre 99 is a thriving improv community that has taken shape in my town. Fifteen years ago, the only people doing improv in Charleston were Brandy, Timmy, and me (The Have Nots!), and now there is a whole tribe of people who don't just watch—they participate in creating improv.

I believe that thriving improv communities can spring up in small-to-midsized cities and towns all across America. It took us over 15 years of doing shows in every bar, theatre, and abandoned storefront in town, but we committed to Charleston, and eventually, Charleston committed to us.

I guess that is what I would like to leave you with. If you love improv and want improv to love you back, then, like in all great love affairs, you have got to commit. Whatever that means to you—commit to the methods in this book, commit to your team or group, commit to getting better at other-focus, commit to believing in the world of the scene, commit to doing improv once a week in your friend's basement, commit to opening a theatre in your town—whatever. Just commit.

If you commit to improv, improv will commit to you.

I fell in love with improv when I was 18, and by committing to the methods in this book, I found a way to get improv to love me back. I hope this book helps you and improv have a long-term, committed relationship because improv has had a very positive effect on me. It has made me more playful with my friends and family. It has made it easier for me to participate in my own life by helping me connect with other people, play with them, and have fun. It has also made me less anxious in social situations because I worry less about other people's judgment of me.

Because improv is in my life, I have more fun and less judgment, and that works for me.

You know you already love improv. Now all you need to do is commit, and improv will love you back.

Greg Tavares

Greg acts, teaches, and directs in Charleston, South Carolina. He did his first improv show in 1985 and has never stopped. In 1995, he cofounded The Have Nots! with Brandy Sullivan and some other friends. He cofounded Theatre 99 in Charleston with Brandy and Timmy Finch in 2000. He wrote the curriculum taught in Theatre 99's training program and gets as much out of teaching as he does from being on stage. He performs and teaches at improv festivals all over the country. He has a BFA in acting from the University of South Carolina and an MFA in directing from the University of Nebraska but still has nightmares that he never finished high school. When he is not acting or directing, he is hanging out with his best friend and wife, Sara, and their son, Lincoln. If you want to reach out to Greg, you can e-mail him at gregtavares99@gmail.com.

Photo: David Mandel

www.ingramcontent.com/pod-product-compliance
Lightning Source LLC
LaVergne TN
LVHW051546070426
835507LV00021B/2435